# COMPUTER-ASSISTED REPORTING
## A PRACTICAL GUIDE

# COMPUTER-ASSISTED REPORTING
## A PRACTICAL GUIDE

**Second Edition**

Brant Houston
INVESTIGATIVE REPORTERS AND EDITORS, INC.
UNIVERSITY OF MISSOURI–COLUMBIA

**Bedford/St. Martin's**
Boston/New York

**For Bedford/St. Martin's**

*Executive Editor:* Patricia Rossi
*Developmental Editor:* Michael Gillespie
*Associate Production Editor:* Jessica Zorn
*Production Supervisor:* Dennis J. Conroy
*Marketing Manager:* Charles Cavaliere
*Art Direction/Cover Design:* Lucy Krikorian
*Text Design:* Patricia McFadden
*Copy Editor:* Patricia Mansfield Phelan
*Indexer:* Riofrancos and Co. Indexes
*Cover Art:* © FPG International LLC
*Composition:* Jan Ewing, Ewing Systems
*Printing and Binding:* R. R. Donnelley Sons & Company

*President:* Charles H. Christensen
*Editorial Director:* Joan E. Feinberg
*Editor in Chief:* Nancy Perry
*Director of Editing, Design, and Production:* Marcia Cohen
*Managing Editor:* Erica T. Appel

Library of Congress Catalog Card Number: 98-84695

Manufactured in the United States of America.

4  3  2  1  0
f  e  d  c  b

*For information, write:* Bedford/St. Martin's, 75 Arlington Street,
Boston, MA 02116    (617-426-7440)

ISBN: 0-312-18852-8

### Acknowledgments

*Acknowledgments and copyrights can be found at the back of the book on
page 216, which constitutes an extension of the copyright page.*

*To all the journalists who
struggle with bits and bytes*

# PREFACE

Continuing advances in computer technology and in the development of powerful software programs have changed the modern newsroom and the way journalists research and write stories. *Computer-Assisted Reporting: A Practical Guide,* Second Edition, is a user-friendly guide that teaches students how to use computers to gather and analyze information more quickly, to provide more context for the data they provide, and to find and develop story ideas from online sources. It covers the basics of computer-assisted reporting (or CAR), providing instruction in the use of database managers, spreadsheets, online resources, beginning statistics, and in the fundamentals of mapping data. And unlike other books in the field, it is written by a journalist who has actually done the work.

*Computer-Assisted Reporting* is a "how-to" introduction to computer-assisted reporting; it can stand alone or serve as a supplement to almost any traditional journalism textbook. The challenge in writing the book has been to simplify complex concepts, to suggest the potential power of certain techniques without getting lost in data or programming, and to show that computer skills can truly improve a journalist's work. During the past five years, I have overseen more than 250 CAR seminars and conferences and taught more than 80 personally, both in print and broadcast journalism, for students as well as professional journalists. As a result, the book's step-by-step approach to computer-assisted reporting is "road-tested," and I have learned how to better teach the subject by listening to suggestions from the thousands of students and professionals who have passed through this training.

## ■≡≡≡ FEATURES

Because computer-assisted reporting requires great attention to detail and repetition of tasks, this book contains many step-by-step instructions, examples, and exercises. Among the key features of the book that have been retained and strengthened in the second edition are:

- A practical, nuts-and-bolts approach that helps students master the basics of computer-assisted reporting, teaching them the essential information and skills they need in clear, understandable language.

- Step-by-step procedures that guide students through the complexities of commonly used software programs, such as Microsoft Excel and Microsoft Access, and Internet sources. Students can match what they see in the book to what they see on their computer screens to confirm they are using the programs correctly.

- Numerous real-life news stories written with the aid of computer-assisted reporting techniques that show students the utility and power of CAR skills.

- Suggested Tasks at the end of each chapter that provide realistic and engaging assignments, giving students an opportunity to practice the skills they learn.

## ■≡≡≡ NEW TO THIS EDITION

The second edition has been thoroughly revised and updated to include discussions of the latest technology available as well as to address changes in the field of computer-assisted reporting. Some of the most significant changes to the second edition are:

- A new chapter on mapping (Chapter 5) that teaches students how to use mapping software to discern and visualize geographical patterns in data, such as locating toxic waste sites within a particular region.

- An updated and expanded chapter on retrieving documents and data online that shows students how to find leads and resources for news stories by using the Internet and other online sources.

- Ready-reference appendices that have been updated and expanded to include lists of helpful Web sites for journalists, advice on compressing and decompressing data files, and information on the legal and ethical issues of computer-assisted reporting.

- An interactive Web site at <http://www.ire.org/carbook> that has been constructed to augment and update *Computer-Assisted Reporting* until its next revision. This Web site will offer exercises and data sets that can be downloaded, brief supplementary tutorials, links to related online sources, and a forum where I can answer questions about the book and its exercises.

The Web site replaces the exercise disk that was included with the first edition of this text. However, if you do not have access to the Internet, a disk may be ordered in either PC or Mac format from Investigative Reporters and Editors (IRE) and the National Institute for Computer-Assisted Reporting (NICAR, which is a joint program of IRE and the Missouri School of Journalism). The exercises can either be shipped to you on disk or sent to you via email. You can contact IRE and NICAR at: IRE/NICAR, 138 Neff Annex, Columbia, Mo 65211; (573) 882-2042; and <info@nicar.org>.

Ultimately, to become proficient at computer-assisted reporting there is no substitute for doing the actual work—finding and negotiating for databases, downloading them from computer tapes or disks, analyzing the data, working through the problems inherent in electronic information, and publishing stories based on that work. However, *Computer-Assisted Reporting* offers the kind of expert, step-by-step guidance that enables students to master the powerful tools of today's newsroom and to gain practical experience in computer-assisted reporting.

## ACKNOWLEDGMENTS

I thank Investigative Reporters and Editors, Inc. (IRE), the Missouri School of Journalism, and Dean Mills for providing pioneering support for computer-assisted reporting; Steve Weinberg, former executive director of IRE and professor at the Missouri School of Journalism, for his support and encouragement; the current and former staff at IRE and the National Institute for Computer-Assisted Reporting (NICAR); the current and former NICAR training directors Jennifer LaFleur, Neil Reisner, and Sarah Cohen; my academic colleague Richard Mullins; and all the journalists and students who have made helpful suggestions, especially Philip Meyer, Nora Paul, and George Landau. At Bedford/St. Martin's, I would like to thank Suzanne Phelps Weir, sponsoring editor; Laura Barthule, editorial assistant; Michael Gillespie, developmental editor; Jessica Zorn, associate production editor; and Scott Lavelle and Dennis Conroy, production supervisors.

I also appreciate the suggestions and help provided by Arin Stark, Jack Dolan, Justin Mayo, and John Sullivan, and by the instructors from across the country who reviewed this book: August Gribbin (Marquette University), Bill Kobarik (Radford University), William Loving (University of Minnesota–Twin Cities), Ed Trayes (Temple University), and Kathleen Wickham (The University of Memphis).

Elliot Jaspin, Philip Meyer, and Dwight Morris, first-generation CAR journalists and mentors, continue to be an inspiration to me. I owe thanks to Elliot for starting in 1989 the organization that has become NICAR and setting the high standards for NICAR's work.

Last, I want to emphasize that despite the power and breadth of computer-assisted reporting, it remains only a tool for journalists. It aids, but does not replace, the imagination, experience, interviewing skills, intuition, skepticism, "shoe leather" work, and passion of the dedicated journalist.

Brant Houston

# CONTENTS

# HIGH-TECH JOURNALISM:
## WHAT COMPUTER-ASSISTED REPORTING IS AND WHY JOURNALISTS NEED TO USE IT

You are looking into the early release of convicts from state prisons because of overcrowding. A good source has told you that many convicts released into a so-called supervised home release program are never supervised at all. In fact, the system loses track of the convicts until they are arrested again.

Prison officials say they don't know if that's true, but they say you can look at individual inmate records if you want to.

Here's the catch: there are 20,000 records.

Prison officials are counting on you having to look at 20,000 sheets of paper. They believe you will give up on the story because it will take you and other reporters months to go through all the records. At best, they think you'll develop some anecdotal evidence they can easily refute.

But you have an answer. You say you'll take the records not on paper but on a computer tape.

After a series of meetings, the officials agree to give you the computer tape with the information you need. You pick up the tape in the morning and transfer the information to your personal computer in the afternoon. By the next morning, using store-bought software, you've determined that more than 1,000 convicts walked away from the program in the past year.

Over the next few days, you check through the records and gather more details. You recheck your information, conduct

1

interviews, and write the story. A week later, you run a front-page story that presents a systematic look at a program gone wrong.

Or try this scenario:

A big-time financier comes to town, driving a Rolls-Royce and talking about investing $40 million in real estate. Bankers excitedly make loans to him, and city officials befriend him.

A few months later, a bank president who made loans to the financier dies in a mysterious car wreck. You are in the midst of writing about the wreck on a Friday afternoon when a source tells you that the financier and an associate were connected to a series of bank failures. The source also tells you that your competition, a weekly business journal, has heard the same thing.

But while your competition is working the phone lines, you are working online. Instead of randomly scattering calls, you check an online nationwide newspaper clipping service and discover that the financier and his associate were indeed linked to bank failures throughout the country.

You check federal bankruptcy court records in various states and find that the associate's corporations have filed for bankruptcy several times, leaving creditors short millions of dollars.

You go on the Internet and search for experts who have dealt with these kinds of schemes. You also check financial filings by the associate's companies with the Securities and Exchange Commission.

While waiting for responses to your search for experts, you go to a Web site containing all the listed phone numbers in the United States and look up the numbers of some of those who have filed suit. You call them, and they tell you the financier is tied to another associate who has been accused of insurance fraud. You go back online and check the federal court records, and there's the case.

Meanwhile, you've gotten three responses from experts, as well as responses to your question about the financial practices. You call the experts for interviews. They say the financier's practices are risky, if not doomed.

With this information, you call board members of the bank whose president has died and tell them what you have learned. They acknowledge that their bank is in trouble because of its loans to the financier.

You call the financier himself. He confirms some of your information, denies a little, and makes excuses for the rest. Your story appears on Sunday, the day before the business journal—your competition—comes out.

Although the outcomes of these two scenarios may exceed the norm, neither of them is far-fetched. In fact, the first scenario actually happened.[1] The second scenario is fictional, but it might have happened if journalists investigating the bank story had been working today instead of in 1983.[2]

The techniques described above are part of an expanding trend in journalism known as computer-assisted reporting (CAR), and they have led to stories that won Pulitzer Prizes or were Pulitzer finalists in the last nine years.

Computer-assisted reporting means that journalists are using computers not only to write stories but to do far-reaching research through online databases; to gather large numbers of records from governmental agencies; to analyze those records; and to use that analysis to launch stories from a higher level and with deeper context than ever before. Computer-assisted reporting doesn't replace proven journalistic practices. It supplements those practices and elevates them. "Verify, verify, verify" becomes ever more critical. "Healthy skepticism" becomes more than idle suspicion.

"Computers don't make a bad reporter into a good reporter. What they do is make a good reporter better," says Elliot Jaspin, one of the pioneers in computer-assisted reporting.[3]

Unfortunately, in the past, many journalists were reluctant to go high-tech because of computer phobia, math phobia, and—until the 1990s—the difficulty and expense of learning

---

[1] Houston, B., and Tuohy, L. Home Release Is "Back Door" to Freedom for Convicts. *Hartford Courant* (Nov. 29, 1992), p. 1.

[2] Numerous articles in the *Kansas City Star* and other newspapers (1982–1983). Also, Pizzo, Stephen, and Fricker, Mary. *Inside Job*. New York, NY. McGraw-Hill, 1989.

[3] Harnessing Computers to Cover the News. *The Forum* (September 1993), p. 6.

how to use computers and computer software. Although some of these barriers remain, they are far lower than they used to be. A powerful number-crunching computer can now be purchased for less than $1,500, and many people use such a computer at home. Small and large news organizations already have such computers, although they often use them only for word processing or pagination. At the same time, software for data analysis is available for less than $100, and software and equipment for online communication often come with the computer. Moreover, the software for personal computers is much easier to learn than it used to be. Numerous reporters have been introduced to spreadsheet software (one of the basic tools of computer-assisted reporting) in an afternoon and have been able to use it effectively for a story within a day or two.

In addition, the language of computers and software and online databases has become less threatening. During the past several years, journalists have had to write about the Internet and the World Wide Web, marketing databases, and CD-ROMs. All this talk and writing have made the technology seem more familiar and sometimes downright friendly.

Computer-assisted reporting, however, is not a sidebar to mainstream journalism. It will be essential to surviving as a journalist in the 21st century. The tools of computer-assisted reporting won't replace a good journalist's imagination, the ability to conduct revealing interviews, or the talent to develop sources. But a journalist who knows how to use computers in day-to-day and long-term work will gather and analyze information more quickly, provide more context, and develop and deliver a deeper understanding of the story's subject.

The journalist also will begin to achieve parity with politicians, bureaucrats, and businesspeople who have enjoyed many advantages over the Fourth Estate simply because they knew how to use computers and electronic information. Governmental officials and workers are generally quite comfortable entering information into computers and then retrieving and analyzing it. Businesses, small and large, routinely use spreadsheet and database software. Political campaign leaders have long scoffed at the inability of many reporters to electronically sort through financial contribution records.

Without a rudimentary knowledge of the advantages and disadvantages of computers, it is difficult for a journalist to understand and report on how the world now works. And it is far more difficult for a journalist to do meaningful public service journalism or to perform the necessary watchdog role.

Frank Daniels III, former executive editor of the *Raleigh News & Observer*, began his newspaper's oft-lauded push into computer-assisted reporting after the 1990 campaign of Senator Jesse Helms proved to be profoundly more computer sophisticated than Daniels's own newspaper. "It made me realize how stupid we were, and I don't like feeling stupid," Daniels recalled in a 1994 interview.[4]

Daniels was right about the bad position in which journalists had put themselves. For years, journalists had been like animals in a zoo, waiting to be fed pellets of information by keepers who were happy to have the journalists stay in their Luddite cages. But now journalists need to learn the basic tools of computer-assisted reporting because it is the best way to get to the information. After all, most governmental and commercial records are now stored electronically, and a huge number of records and databases are available through the World Wide Web. Without the ability to deal with electronic data, a journalist is choosing to catch a ride rather than drive on the information superhighway. The old-fashioned journalist will never get to the destination on time—or worse, will be brutally run over by the competing media. Furthermore, a good journalist wants to see original documents or exact copies of those documents. Every time a journalist lets someone else select or sort those documents, he or she risks letting someone else add a spin or bias that can't be detected.

A journalist who can use a spreadsheet or database manager is free to thoroughly explore documents, to reexamine them, and to reconsider what the documents mean in relation to interviews and observations in the field. If a journalist lets a data processor do the analysis, the nuances or potential pitfalls of the data may be missed. A data processor does not think like

---

[4] Moeller, P. The Digitized Newsroom. *American Journalism Review* (January/February 1995), p. 44.

a journalist; what may be significant to the journalist may seem unimportant to the data processor. Using a data processor to do all the work is like asking someone else to read a book for you.

The good journalist also does not want to fall into a cycle of asking for a printout, studying the printout, coming up with more questions, and then asking for another printout. Why get into a lengthy discussion with a data processor when you can personally engage in a rapid conversation with the data on a computer screen?

Finally, another good reason to learn CAR tools is to be able to tell when someone else is misusing them. A journalist may not be a statistician, but a good journalist knows enough about statistics to realize how easy it is to manipulate or lie with them. In the same way, if a journalist understands how data can be manipulated, he or she can better judge a bureaucrat's spin on the facts or a government's misuse of a database.

Most important, computer-assisted reporting is at the heart of good public service journalism.

## ▦▦▦ The Basic Tools

Over the past decade, three basic tools for computer-assisted reporting have emerged: spreadsheets, database managers, and online resources. As journalists have become more sophisticated, other tools—including mapping software and statistical software—have joined these three. In providing training to thousands of journalists, the National Institute for Computer-Assisted Reporting has found that the beginning journalist in computer-assisted reporting starts most comfortably with the first three tools.

*Spreadsheet software* is good for analyzing numbers. Think about using a spreadsheet whenever you are looking at salaries, budgets, census data, prices, or statistical reports. A spreadsheet allows you to add columns of numbers quickly, compare them, sort them, and chart your results. Of course, a spreadsheet can allow you to do much more; but for basic computer-assisted reporting, this is its routine use.

A *database manager* is good for keeping track of sources; it works better than a paper Rolodex or index cards. A database manager can group similar kinds of information and link different files through keywords or identification numbers. It enables you to look up information about a person quickly by name, street address, or phone number. It allows you to look up political contributions to a particular candidate, group those contributions, and total them. It lets you match the names in one file of information, such as death certificates, to names in another file, such as voters. (There's always a potential story when you find dead people voting.) A database manager also can handle many more records than a spreadsheet because spreadsheets technically are limited to 64,000 records. As a practical matter, however, working with more than a few thousand records in a spreadsheet can be awkward.

*Online resources* are available to journalists who can contact another computer through a modem (a device that allows one computer to phone another) or through a network in which computers are already linked. Online resources include:

1. *electronic mail (email),* by which people can send messages to—and receive messages from—people all over the world

2. *discussion groups*—known as listservs—on certain subjects

3. *database libraries,* where sets of records are stored

4. *bulletin boards*—often called newsgroups—where people can post messages to be read by anyone who drops by

With online resources, you can look up court records, retrieve thousands of campaign records or the federal budget, dial into your local city hall, or find experts a continent away.

*Mapping software* helps illustrate the points made in a story and sometimes illuminates disclosures that otherwise would remain unseen. *Statistical software* becomes attractive later when a journalist feels more comfortable with numbers and wants to perform more detailed analysis.

Computer-assisted reporting uses other tools, some of which are complex and some of which are merely handy. Certainly, more sophisticated journalists are using higher-level statistics and complicated parts of mapping software, but this handbook will concentrate on the basic tools and analysis that can get you going. It will strip away the distractions (such as computer manuals) that seem so plentiful when you begin learning how to use software, and it will show you shortcuts to doing effective stories.

This handbook also will try to help you understand how computers operate and how their designers think. Working with computers requires a different way of thinking. It is more methodical and initially less intuitive, but the rewards are better skills and better stories.

## ▇▤▤▤ Trial and Error, and Repetition

The best way to learn computer-assisted reporting is through trial and error. *You have to practice.* You have to make mistakes in asking questions of the information. You need to try different queries in database managers, look at the result, and try again. The exercises (they can be found on the Web or ordered in diskette form) will give you plenty of opportunity to try different ways of arranging data and to discover the best way to find valid answers. Moreover, you have to realize that despite the improvements, computer software still has quirks and obscure keystrokes. Practice and more practice is the way to become more comfortable with the tools.

## ▇▤▤▤ Where You're Going

This handbook provides an overview of how to do computer-assisted reporting in what may seem like a reverse order. Usually, a journalist obtains data from a governmental agency, enters the data into a computer, puts the data into a spreadsheet or database manager, and then uses software to examine the information.

However, this handbook starts by examining in Chapter 2 some general principles of the operation of computers and the different way of thinking required of a journalist who uses computers. Then, the handbook discusses the use of software to examine the information contained in electronic databases, how to negotiate with governmental agencies so they will give you the information, and how to find and correct errors contained in the information. Instructors throughout the country have found this order of instruction to be a logical way of explaining computer-assisted reporting to journalists.

Journalists and students are practical people who want to see the point of a new technique before they invest a lot of time in learning it. If journalists and students realize that they can analyze thousands of campaign finance records in an hour instead of two weeks, they will likely become interested in learning how to transfer those records from a disk into a computer. Therefore, Chapter 3 introduces spreadsheets, which most journalists agree are the fundamental tool for starting out in computer-assisted analysis. Spreadsheets usually deal with a limited number of records organized in columns and rows of information.

Chapter 4 describes the basic uses of database managers, which can be a bit more difficult to learn. As previously mentioned, these are frequently used for grouping categories of records and for linking one file of information to another. Database managers allow you to select columns of information, filter in or filter out certain kinds of information, group some items together, and then order the results. In addition, you may link one file of information in a database to another, or do what is sometimes called matchmaking. Chapter 4 will focus on these principles.

Chapter 5 shows some simple uses of mapping software in which a journalist can visually identify and locate items such as environmental toxic sites or building violations; outline patterns of possible discrimination based on neighborhood, income, or ethnicity; and demonstrate trends that might pass unnoticed.

Chapter 6 explores descriptive statistics and techniques that a journalist can use to avoid the smaller perils when looking at databases. As journalists use computers more, they are starting to apply social research techniques in their reporting. Thus, journalists need to know some of the basic measures of information. They also need to know how not to stray into the dangerous territory of assumptions, thinking that correlation equals cause. The basic technique examined in Chapter 6 is the use of descriptive statistics. The chapter also demonstrates the use of crosstabs, which are quick ways of counting and finding percentages.

Chapters 7 examines online resources, primarily those found on the World Wide Web and put together by government agencies. This is a broad area, because online resources reflect the vastness of our world. The advent of the World Wide Web, which allows transfer not only of text and data but also of sound and video, is regarded by many as the great leap forward for the Internet. Instead of being confused by detailed programming lines, a journalist can simply use a mouse to point and click on words or images about which he or she wants to know more.

Many journalists are still struggling to use the online world for news stories, although disasters such as airline crashes, earthquakes in California and Japan, and the terrorist bombing in Oklahoma City have shown why journalists should pay close attention to the online world. This handbook describes a few techniques for navigating in cyberspace, concentrating on concepts that help you pinpoint what you need. Many books are devoted wholly to online services and the Internet, and you can research those for more specific information. This handbook deals with the use of information you find for stories, both on deadline and for longer pieces.

Chapter 8 considers the art of finding and negotiating for databases. Because the laws in many states are only beginning to catch up with technology, problems with obtaining databases for reasonable prices abound. This chapter examines some of the obstacles presented by bureaucrats and commercial vendors and advises you on how to get around them.

Chapter 9 looks at the pitfalls of "dirty" databases. Most, if not all, databases contain errors (just like newspapers and TV reports). A journalist needs to know how to find those errors and either correct them or note them. The cleaning up of dirty data can become complex, but Chapter 9 touches on some of the basic methods.

Chapter 10 talks about strategies for getting started on computer-assisted stories and how not to get lost in the abundance of information and possibilities.

The software packages used to illustrate examples in this handbook include the spreadsheet program Microsoft Excel, the database manager Microsoft Access, the statistical package SPSS, the mapping software ArcView, and several online vendors and searchers. The particular packages and services were chosen because of their wide use by journalists and because of their convenience to the author. The author doesn't endorse any specific one. Moreover, the handbook's appendices contain the names of other software that journalists can use. When learning computer-assisted reporting, you need to find software that is easy for you to acquire and understand and that gets the job done.

## ■■≡≡ PRACTICAL ADVICE

Computer-assisted reporting is a new adventure with a multitude of possibilities. This handbook does not attempt to cover everything; instead, it offers enough practical advice to jumpstart the hesitant student or journalist into using it for daily, beat, or long-term reporting. Furthermore, a journalist's success in learning computer-assisted reporting depends on that journalist's own efforts. It's a lot like the old lightbulb joke:

How many psychiatrists does it take to change a lightbulb?

One.

But the lightbulb has to really want to change.

## ■■≡≡ CHAPTER SUMMARY

❏ Journalists need to know how to search for and analyze information on computers because governments, businesses, political campaigns, and the like use computers to store and distribute information.

❏ The three basic tools of computer-assisted reporting are spreadsheets, database managers, and online resources. More sophisticated tools include mapping software and statistical software.

❏ Once learned, computer-assisted reporting permits a journalist to quickly gather ever more comprehensive information.

❏ The best way to learn computer-assisted reporting is through trial and error, and repetition.

## ■≡ Suggested Tasks

❏ Identify three Pulitzer Prize–winning news stories that used computer-assisted reporting to analyze government databases. Explain how those stories were done.

❏ Identify three breaking news stories and follow-up stories that used computer-assisted reporting. Find explanations of how those stories were done.

❏ Identify three stories that used or could use spreadsheet software.

❏ Identify three stories that used or could use a database manager.

❏ Identify three stories that used or could use online resources.

❏ Identify three stories that used or could use mapping software.

❏ Identify three stories that used or could use statistical software.

❏ Find database managers (such as Microsoft Access) and spreadsheet software (such as Microsoft Excel), and open those programs to see what they look like.

*Hint:* All the resources necessary to answer these questions are available at the Web sites of Investigative Reporters and Editors at <http://www.ire.org> and the National Institute for Computer-Assisted Reporting at <http://www.nicar.org>.

# Computer Basics: Translating the Technical into the Practical

Journalists are used to running to a press conference, firing questions at a spokesperson, running back to the office, frantically making phone calls while writing a story, and then trying to check a few key facts before the story is published or aired.

If you are delving into a database or going online to find information, you need to switch to a lower gear and apply the brakes. Indeed, a computer requires you to plan ahead, to work more slowly, and to pause and consider what you have done.

For example, computer software takes your typographical mistakes very seriously. To a piece of software, a misplaced comma or a blank space can distort the result of a question you have posed. Sometimes, 90 percent of computer-assisted reporting seems to involve typing accurately or clicking a mouse correctly. Using a computer mouse doesn't eliminate the need for precision, because it's just as easy to click on the wrong item. And even when you use a mouse, you will, at some point, still have to type.

You may think you don't have the time to be this precise, but you do. In fact, spending a few extra seconds being careful can save you hours of toil and trouble.

## ▉▤ COLUMNS AND ROWS

As journalists, we deal with text-long strings of letters and words that run from line to line to the end of the screen. When we get to the end of one screen, we keep on typing to the next screen. Everything pours out in one long scroll. But in the computer-assisted reporting world, text is often the last thing we use. Before we get to text, we have to do our research and analysis.

What do we work with instead of text? We work with columns and rows of information. Richard Mullins, an assistant professor at the Missouri School of Journalism and a respected teacher of computer-assisted reporting, likes to call this the "two-dimensional world." Although many journalists initially resist this way of looking at information on a computer screen, we're all familiar with it. We not only use phone directories and city directories, but we put columns and rows in our own work. This kind of information is also known as "tabular," because its columns and rows are called "tables."

In any newspaper, we find pages and pages of columns and rows, or tabular information. In the front section of the *New York Times*, you might find several charts of names and numbers dealing with such things as hog farms, taxes, census studies, and budgets. In the business section, there might be four or five pages of columns and rows detailing stocks, bonds, and mutual funds. In the sports section, you might see the scores of professional and college teams, and statistics on individual athletes.

We ponder the two-dimensional world every day. If we're interested in sports, for example, we check the rankings of teams. Table 2-1 shows such a ranking. The first column contains the rank; the second, the team's name; the third, the team's win-loss record.

| TABLE 2-1 | | |
|-----------|----------|--------|
| *Rank* | *Team* | *Record* |
| 1 | Nebraska | 10-0 |
| 2 | Texas | 9-1 |
| 3 | Florida | 9-1 |
| 4 | Miami | 8-2 |

As you can see in Table 2-1, the columns are categories of information, and each row (also known as a *record*) gives information for each category for a particular team. Most journalists have written by hand many lists that contain columns and rows. But it's easy to lose a list, and if it gets too long, it's not easy to sort. Columns and rows on paper are petrified information.

Keeping such information electronically makes it flexible. With software tools, you can change the order of the columns and rows. With electronic information, you can reconstruct the list in Table 2-1 and arrange it in the format shown in Table 2-2.

**TABLE 2-2**

| Team | Record | Rank |
|------|--------|------|
| Miami | 8-2 | 4 |
| Florida | 9-1 | 3 |
| Texas | 9-1 | 2 |
| Nebraska | 10-0 | 1 |

Although the sorting in Table 2-2 may not seem particularly useful (unless you're looking for the team with the lowest ranking), the ability to manipulate information by different categories and in a different order is valuable.

Journalists frequently want to discover how much public employee salaries are costing taxpayers. The information regarding people's salaries has at least three categories: name, title, and salary. Each row is a record of each person's information. Look at Table 2-3.

**TABLE 2-3**

| Name | Title | Salary |
|------|-------|--------|
| Josephine Smith | Comptroller | $54,000 |
| Juan Hinojosa | City Manager | $72,000 |
| James Brown | Purchasing Agent | $44,000 |
| Joan Bertrand | Parks Administrator | $48,000 |

With a spreadsheet or database manager, you can look at a list and sort it quickly, as you can with sports standings. In Table 2-4, we put the top-salaried person at the top of the list.

| TABLE 2-4 | | |
| --- | --- | --- |
| *Name* | *Title* | *Salary* |
| Juan Hinojosa | City Manager | $72,000 |
| Josephine Smith | Comptroller | $54,000 |
| Joan Bertrand | Parks Administrator | $48,000 |
| James Brown | Purchasing Agent | $44,000 |

Whether a list consists of four names or a thousand, it doesn't matter to a spreadsheet or a database manager.

## ■▦ OPERATING SYSTEMS

If you want to drive a car, you need to know a little about its mechanics. You don't need to know how to take apart the engine, but you do need to know that the steering wheel turns the tires and that the accelerator controls how fast the car goes. In the same way, to use a computer, you need to know something about its mechanics.

This handbook assumes that you can turn on a computer and its screen. It also assumes that you can use a keyboard and a mouse, but it does not assume that you know how a file is stored or retrieved. To understand how to open a file, you need to know a little about the operating system. An *operating system* organizes software programs and information in a computer. Consider it a relentless administrative assistant.

Among operating systems, there is DOS (an old one). Then there are the different versions of Windows, which puts a friendly face on DOS and has icons that look a lot like those on Apple computers. There is Macintosh, which came before Windows. And there is Unix, and then there is . . .

What do you really need to know?

You'll have to know which operating system runs your computer and which key commands make it run. This handbook won't try to teach you how to run operating systems, but it will give you a few principles. A good book about your computer's operating system, a patient colleague, or both can give you enough clues so that you'll be able to work on your computer in a matter of an hour or two.

## ■■≡≡ Boxes Inside Boxes

No matter which operating system your computer uses, its thinking can be symbolized by Russian nesting dolls. You may remember these dolls from childhood. The first doll is as large as your hand, but it's built in two parts that fit together; pull the top half from the bottom half and there is another doll inside; pull that doll apart, and you find another one inside; and so on. That's how computers organize information—as boxes inside boxes inside boxes.

Say you have information about city hall. A computer would like you to keep all your information about city hall in a box called "cityhall." But you might have so much information on city hall that it's hard to find it quickly. So, within the box "cityhall," you create another box, "budget." But that box might still have too much information. So, you create a bunch of boxes within "budget" called "fire," "law," "police," "zoning," and so on.

Your computer might represent your city hall data as file folders within file folders, or through a map that is referred to as a *tree* or *path*. A path is like a railroad line. You can't get from "cityhall" to "zoning" without going through "budget." Table 2-5 shows what your storage structure would look like in a Windows operating system.

**TABLE 2-5**

What makes life confusing for a journalist is that different operating systems use different names for storage: subdirectories, databases, folders, workbooks. Don't be confused. Once you know your system's particular lingo, you will know what to call these boxes and will be able to easily retrieve stored information.

## ▣▤ Technospeak

Speaking of lingo, we need to briefly discuss certain areas of technospeak.

Information often goes onto a *hard drive* or a *disk* or a *CD-ROM.* These storage areas are best imagined as compact disks (CDs), except they don't hold tunes. Instead, they hold the greatest hits, for example, of federal elections or Federal Aviation Administration reports or employee injury reports.

A *hard drive* is a disk inside a computer on which electronic files are stored. A *diskette,* or *floppy disk,* is generally a 3.5-inch-square plastic disk that holds electronic files. The square itself is hard plastic, but if you open it up (don't do this if you plan to use it), you will find a floppy disk of plastic inside. To use the diskette, you first insert it into a slot in the computer.

*CD-ROM* stands for *compact disk, read-only memory. Read only* means that once electronic information is put on the CD, it cannot be written to again. You can "overwrite" information, however, on a hard drive and on a disk or tape.

Storage space is measured in *bytes;* each byte is composed of eight *bits.* A byte is best imagined as a character—for example, as the letter *A* or the number *6.* A common floppy disk can contain about 1.4 million bytes—or the equivalent of several books. Most current hard drives contain a thousand million bytes (a gigabyte) or more. A CD-ROM can contain more than 600 million bytes—that is 600 megabytes. (Note we use the term *megabytes* for "a million bytes" and *gigabyte* for "a billion bytes.") Although this seems like an enormous amount, it's amazing how rapidly a good journalist can fill up a hard drive with software and data.

Next, there is *RAM,* or *random-access memory,* the place on the computer where programs and files are temporarily stored.

Think of RAM as a desk where you can lay out papers to be collated or stapled. Journalists are always short of desk space. Well, computers are usually short of desk space, too. All the software that puts icons and graphics on your computer screen greedily eats up space. In any case, RAM comes in much smaller amounts of megabytes, varying from 16 megabytes on older computers to 64 megabytes or more on newer computers. Usually, about 32 to 64 megabytes of RAM are needed to run the newest programs.

So, there are two places in a computer where you have to worry about space: the hard drive and the RAM.

In general, you should try to keep as much of your storage space as free as you can. If you run out of storage space on your hard drive, you will have to discard some data files before you can use the computer. It's the same idea as having a full file cabinet when you need to store more files.

Many operating systems try to keep the RAM (or worktable space) as open as possible. However, if you run out of RAM, your computer will usually freeze up and send incomprehensible error messages, or "crash." If this happens, your only hope will be to either restart the computer or find a knowledgeable colleague who can help you clear more space in your RAM.

There is another crucial difference between storage on the hard drive and storage in the RAM. When you exit a software program or shut down the machine, the computer acts as a fanatical janitor and sweeps your RAM clean. Unlike a newsroom, where you can build pyramids of paper on your desk, a computer runs a tight ship.

This brings us to the cardinal rule of every computer system: constantly save your work. Always keep backup copies. Save to a hard drive, and save to a disk. Never trust the computer to save for you. *Do* trust the computer to lose everything you have not saved when a power failure occurs or a piece of software goes wacky.

Are there other reasons why you should care about megabytes on the hard drive or in the RAM? Well, if you want to get a file (let's call it a database) from the government, you need to know whether you can transfer it to your hard drive. If the database requires 50 megabytes of space and there are only 25 megabytes left on your hard drive, you're in trouble. You'll have to get rid of outdated or unnecessary information on the hard drive to make room for the new.

Then, if you want to look at the database with your spreadsheet or database manager software, you need to make sure that the software doesn't require 32 megabytes of RAM when you have only 16. Without the additional RAM, the software won't run.

Don't worry too much about megabytes now; we will return to them later in the book.

## ■▤▤ MODEMS AND NETWORKS

Unfortunately, you need to know a little about one of the clunkiest devices in the computer world: the modem. Most beginners (and even advanced users) get frustrated by the modem.

A *modem* is supposed to connect your computer to another modem so your computer can "talk" to another computer—that is, so your computer can send (or receive) information, stories, or comments to (or from) another computer. Conceptually, this is as simple as the idea of two children playing telephone by using two tin cans connected by a piece of string. Practically speaking, a modem sometimes works about as well as that.

Connecting modems need to speak the same language at the same speed with the same etiquette. Thus, you have to be extremely careful with the settings on your modem, or a straightforward conversation can turn into what seems like negotiations between two foreign countries.

Modem speed is measured by bits per second (bps). Considering the amount of graphics online now, which use lots of bits, you should get the fastest modem you can afford. A modem that runs at 28,800 bps has been the standard, but there will probably be a new standard by the time you read this book. Be sure that your modem speed is compatible with that of the modem you are trying to call; note that a faster modem can usually slow down to talk to a lower-speed modem.

Sometimes, other conditions have to be met. You may need to know the following quirky settings: N-8-1 or E-7-1. These two settings (which refer to parity, data bits, and stop bits) affect how the bits, or information, are transferred over a line. (Happily, with the newest communication software, you may not need to know any of this.)

*Parity, data bits,* and *start and stop bits* are all important because a single byte of information has to be sent serially across phone lines. As you may recall, a byte is made up of eight bits. Because a messy phone line can turn a byte into nonsense, you need a way of ensuring that the whole byte gets through.

*Start and stop bits* tell the receiving modem that a byte is about to arrive or that it has just arrived. So a start bit says, "Here comes the byte," and the stop bit says, "The byte has been sent."

*Parity* is a way of checking that the entire byte has arrived unscrambled. This brings you to the land of 1s and 0s, or bits, where every byte is composed of a combination of 1s and 0s. The first 128 characters represented by bytes (A through Z, numbers 1–9, and the other characters that appear on your computer screen) use only seven bits, with the eighth bit unnecessary. But people who put together telecommunications software sometimes use that eighth bit as a parity bit.

A parity bit can be used to signify what the rest of a byte should look like. If the byte the parity bit signifies doesn't match the byte received, then the receiving modem knows that there has been an error in transmission.

In short, if you run into problems when trying to contact another modem, you should go down the software checklist of settings. If that doesn't work, get a savvy friend to help you.

Online life becomes more complicated when you try to connect to the Internet. Sometimes, you need a special connection, known as a SLIP (Serial Line Internet Protocol) or PPP (Point to Point Protocol), to get to the Internet through a modem. Like foreign countries, computers need a common language in order to talk to each other.

Commercial services, such as the America Online service, have made it easier to avoid much of this rigmarole. Such services provide easy-to-use software that leads you to the proper settings, and they smooth the path to the Internet, including the eye-pleasing World Wide Web. By the time this handbook is published, connecting to the Internet will be even easier. (How bad the online traffic jams will continue to be is another question.)

Many journalists avoid the perils of the modem by using university or newsroom networks. These networks have easy setups, as well as full-time staff to protect you from the technical pains of communication. When using these networks, you move the mouse, point at an icon, click, and that resource opens up. For example, the *Wisconsin State Journal* in Madison set up icons on a computer screen that allowed journalists to tap into databases at the University of Wisconsin, the Federal Election Commission, and several other locations. "Bookmarks" on Web-browsing software now make it easier for people to find favorite locations on the Web. Meanwhile, many news organizations are busy setting up easy-to-use internal Internet systems called Intranets.

## ■▬ A Helpful Hint

When you start computer-assisted reporting, treat it as a news assignment. Get a notebook, and keep a log of what you have learned each day, especially the technical aspects. This will help you keep track of what you have learned, save you time, and put a damper on your frustration. There's just too much to remember otherwise.

## ■▬ Chapter Summary

- ❑ Electronic information is often arranged in a two-dimensional world of columns and rows.
- ❑ Electronic information is stored in boxes within boxes.
- ❑ Megabytes are a way of measuring storage and work space on a computer.
- ❑ Keep a daily log of what you learn.

## ■≡ Suggested Tasks

❐ Find five examples of columns and rows or tabular information in a newspaper. *Hint:* Check the sports and business pages.

❐ Look at the structure of how electronic files are stored on a computer, and create several folders inside one folder. Place a file in one folder, and then move it to another folder. Then move it back.

❐ Find five examples of tabular information on the World Wide Web. *Hint:* Go to census and economic sites.

❐ Keep a log of the tasks you just performed.

# SPREADSHEETS: CONQUERING NUMBERS

SLOW FIRE RESPONSES FUEL DISASTER WORRIES; FORCE FAILS TO MATCH CITY GROWTH

Even before the sun rose last Wednesday, the day had become one that San Jose firefighters fear.

Confronted with a string of six fires downtown, the fire department—one of the most thinly staffed big-city departments in the country—wasn't keeping up. As new alarms continued to ring, it was taking firefighters longer and longer to respond. When one building roared into an inferno, residents had to jump from a second-floor apartment as it took firefighters 12 minutes to arrive—2½ times as long as it normally should have.[1]

With this headline and these two paragraphs, the *San Jose Mercury News* launched a story into the city fire department's inability to get to fires quickly. Much of the analysis was based on number crunching done on one of the simplest software tools: the spreadsheet.

To prepare the story, reporters Christopher Schmitt and Betty Barnacle obtained an electronic file from the city that included the times of the alarms and the times fire trucks

---

[1] Schmitt, C. H., and Barnacle, B. Mercury News Report: Playing with Fire? *San Jose Mercury News* (March 5, 1989), p. 1A.

24

arrived at the scene. The fire department claimed that its average response time was 4.5 minutes, half a minute under the maximum time it allowed itself to get to any fire.

Schmitt, who did the analysis, found that the fire department was right about its average. However, what the fire department didn't say—but the numbers showed—was that on one-fourth of its calls, the fire department took longer than 5 minutes to respond. Schmitt then wrote a story that revealed a pattern of problems, not just an isolated occurrence.

Spreadsheets are one of the least complex types of software for analysis, and they have been used for both on-the-beat stories and long-term investigations. Schmitt was able to pull together the fire department story in less than a week when a series of arsons hit San Jose, because he already had the database in hand.

*National Law Journal* reporters used spreadsheets while researching an examination of racism and environmental pollution. *Fortune* magazine staffers used spreadsheets in a major wage study. Many newspapers have used spreadsheets to analyze crime statistics, drug arrests, governmental corruption, property taxes, and municipal budgets.

## ■▬▬ BECOMING FRIENDLY WITH NUMBERS

Journalists constantly report on numbers, although you'll often hear them say they hated math in school—and still hate it. Well, many people hate flying on airplanes, but they fly because their jobs require them to. They know the plane will take them where they need to go and will take them there quickly. But not many of them become pilots.

The same idea applies to modern journalists and spreadsheets. Modern journalists don't have to be mathematicians to deal with numbers, but they should be willing to use spreadsheets to get the job done. Journalists report on city budgets, housing costs, and salary raises. Yet, it is startling how many reporters strain for hours with pencil and paper—or even a calculator—to figure out whether the mayor has given his cronies the largest raises.

Eric Lipton, a Pulitzer Prize–winning reporter who now works for the *Washington Post*, discovered the efficiency of spreadsheets while working at the *Hartford Courant*. Lipton was examining a generous early-retirement plan for city employees. Experts told him each pension should equal approximately 67 percent of the employee's salary at the time of retirement.

Lipton was tediously tapping a calculator, comparing each retiree's salary and pension individually, when he remembered that he had seen a spreadsheet demonstration in which calculations were done much more rapidly. With a little help, he imported the information into a spreadsheet and learned how to do one calculation. Then he copied that calculation for more than a hundred other entries. Those calculations served as the starting point for a front-page story, because in doing them, Lipton had discovered that some retirees' pensions came close to 100 percent of their former salaries.

What Lipton learned is that a spreadsheet saves an enormous amount of time, prevents unnecessary repetition, and improves accuracy in calculations.

A spreadsheet allows you to quickly figure out such things as who got the most money, who got the highest percentage raise, who made the most drug arrests, or which city's housing prices increased the most.

Take a look at how a spreadsheet can be used for examining pay raises. You know the average raise for city employees this year is 5 percent. At the same time, you have a list of the mayor's political appointments. Journalists often line up information like this on paper. (If they don't, a graphics department will make them do it.) Table 3-1 shows a partial list of the mayor's cronies on the city payroll. (All names in this example are fictional.)

| TABLE 3-1 | | |
|---|---|---|
| *Name* | *Last year* | *This year* |
| Dee Dale | 45000 | 52000 |
| Ed Powell | 25000 | 30000 |
| Jane Deed | 14000 | 19000 |
| Joe Smith | 30000 | 39000 |
| Julia Jones | 50000 | 58000 |
| Mark Forest | 15000 | 21000 |
| Mary Hill | 22000 | 29000 |
| Tom Brown | 40000 | 47000 |

If we add dollar signs, commas, and gridlines, which make it easier to keep track of the numbers, the information would look like that shown in Table 3-2.

| TABLE 3-2 | | |
|---|---|---|
| *Name* | *Last year* | *This year* |
| Dee Dale | $  45,000 | $  52,000 |
| Ed Powell | $  25,000 | $  30,000 |
| Jane Deed | $  14,000 | $  19,000 |
| Joe Smith | $  30,000 | $  39,000 |
| Julia Jones | $  50,000 | $  58,000 |
| Mark Forest | $  15,000 | $  21,000 |
| Mary Hill | $  22,000 | $  29,000 |
| Tom Brown | $  40,000 | $  47,000 |

A spreadsheet takes this idea a step further. When a spreadsheet takes in information, it arranges it in the kind of grid shown in Table 3-3.

**TABLE 3-3**

| | A | B | C | |
|---|---|---|---|---|
| **1** | Name | Last year | This year | |
| **2** | | | | |
| **3** | Dee Dale | $  45,000 | $  52,000 | |
| **4** | Ed Powell | $  25,000 | $  30,000 | |
| **5** | Jane Deed | $  14,000 | $  19,000 | |
| **6** | Joe Smith | $  30,000 | $  39,000 | |
| **7** | Julia Jones | $  50,000 | $  58,000 | |
| **8** | Mark Forest | $  15,000 | $  21,000 | |
| **9** | Mary Hill | $  22,000 | $  29,000 | |
| **10** | Tom Brown | $  40,000 | $  47,000 | |

As you can see, the only major change in Table 3-3 is that the columns are labeled with letters and the rows with numbers. The letters and rows are the key concept of a spreadsheet, and it's one that you've used in other parts of life.

## ▣▤▤ LEARNING ADDRESSES

If you have ever tried to find a town on a road atlas, you have probably consulted the index. The index may have referred you to page 7 and to the town's location at "D4." You went to page 7. The map was laid out on a grid with letters across the top and numbers down the side. You looked down column D and then looked across row 4 to find the town.

Perhaps you've played chess and want to replay the game. The locations of the chess pieces are also given with letters and numbers. A knight, for example, will move from square B1 to square C3.

Better yet, you may have played the game of Battleship, in which you make a grid with letters and numbers. You strategically place your ships on the grid, thereby blocking consecutive squares. Your opponent does the same. Then you take turns trying to sink your opponent's ships, saying such things as "A4" or "B5." Your opponent says "hit" if one of their ships is on that particular square and "miss" if you hit nothing.

Spreadsheets treat your information as though it's part of a game of Battleship. Spreadsheets generally see a salary not only as $45,000, but also as "B3."

Now, back to the raises and the mayor's cronies.

In Table 3-3, look at the first row. It should show that Dee Dale's salary increased from $45,000 to $52,000. The increase isn't hard to see. It's $7,000.

A journalist normally analyzes raises by taking a calculator and subtracting the information in column B from that in column C. It doesn't take long to do the calculations for 10 or 20 names, but frequently a journalist is handed a list of hundreds or thousands of names. In Lipton's study of pensions and salaries, for example, he had more than 100 names, and he was not happy about the hours of work that lay ahead.

This is where a spreadsheet comes in handy. In a spreadsheet, you would not subtract 45,000 from 52,000. Remember, a spreadsheet is like Battleship. You would subtract B3 from C3, and you would put the result in the blank space next to C3, called D3.

So, here's the way to do it in a spreadsheet. As shown in Table 3-4, you move the cursor to box D3 and click on your mouse. Then you type: "=C3–B3." You type the "=" sign first so that the spreadsheet knows a formula is coming.

**TABLE 3-4**

| SUM | ▼ ✗ ✓ = | =C3-B3 | |
|---|---|---|---|
| | A | B | C | D |
| 1 | Name | Last year | This year | Change |
| 2 | | | | |
| 3 | Dee Dale | $ 45,000 | $ 52,000 | =C3-B3 |
| 4 | Ed Powell | $ 25,000 | $ 30,000 | |
| 5 | Jane Deed | $ 14,000 | $ 19,000 | |
| 6 | Joe Smith | $ 30,000 | $ 39,000 | |
| 7 | Julia Jones | $ 50,000 | $ 58,000 | |
| 8 | Mark Forest | $ 15,000 | $ 21,000 | |
| 9 | Mary Hill | $ 22,000 | $ 29,000 | |
| 10 | Tom Brown | $ 40,000 | $ 47,000 | |

Then you hit the "Enter" key, and there's the result in D3 in Table 3-5: $7,000.

**TABLE 3-5**

| | A | B | C | D |
|---|---|---|---|---|
| 1 | Name | Last year | This year | Change |
| 2 | | | | |
| 3 | Dee Dale | $ 45,000 | $ 52,000 | $ 7,000 |
| 4 | Ed Powell | $ 25,000 | $ 30,000 | |
| 5 | Jane Deed | $ 14,000 | $ 19,000 | |
| 6 | Joe Smith | $ 30,000 | $ 39,000 | |
| 7 | Julia Jones | $ 50,000 | $ 58,000 | |
| 8 | Mark Forest | $ 15,000 | $ 21,000 | |
| 9 | Mary Hill | $ 22,000 | $ 29,000 | |
| 10 | Tom Brown | $ 40,000 | $ 47,000 | |

What you have done is set up a formula—not a complicated one, but a formula nonetheless—that does the simple arithmetic for you.

Now you're ready to use the spreadsheet to save time. You want to repeat the formula for every raise. You repeat the formula by copying, not $7,000, but "=C3–B3." One way to do this is to highlight the formula by placing the cursor on the formula and clicking on it. You then move the cursor to the lower right-hand corner of D3 until you see a narrow cross, as in Table 3-6.

**TABLE 3-6**

| D3 | ▼ | ≡ | =C3-B3 | |
|---|---|---|---|---|
| | A | B | C | D |
| 1 | Name | Last year | This year | Change |
| 2 | | | | |
| 3 | Dee Dale | $ 45,000 | $ 52,000 | $ 7,000 |
| 4 | Ed Powell | $ 25,000 | $ 30,000 | |
| 5 | Jane Deed | $ 14,000 | $ 19,000 | |
| 6 | Joe Smith | $ 30,000 | $ 39,000 | |
| 7 | Julia Jones | $ 50,000 | $ 58,000 | |
| 8 | Mark Forest | $  15,000 | $ 21,000 | |
| 9 | Mary Hill | $ 22,000 | $ 29,000 | |
| 10 | Tom Brown | $ 40,000 | $ 47,000 | |

Next, define or shade the area you want to copy to by clicking on D3, holding down the button on your mouse, and dragging the shading to the last row, as shown in Table 3-7.

**TABLE 3-7**

| D3 | ▼ | ≡ | =C3-B3 | |
|---|---|---|---|---|
| | A | B | C | D |
| 1 | Name | Last year | This year | Change |
| 2 | | | | |
| 3 | Dee Dale | $ 45,000 | $ 52,000 | $ 7,000 |
| 4 | Ed Powell | $ 25,000 | $ 30,000 | |
| 5 | Jane Deed | $ 14,000 | $ 19,000 | |
| 6 | Joe Smith | $ 30,000 | $ 39,000 | |
| 7 | Julia Jones | $ 50,000 | $ 58,000 | |
| 8 | Mark Forest | $ 15,000 | $ 21,000 | |
| 9 | Mary Hill | $ 22,000 | $ 29,000 | |
| 10 | Tom Brown | $ 40,000 | $ 47,000 | |

Note that the top line in Table 3-7 shows the spreadsheet does not see $7,000 in D3, but instead sees "=C3–B3." Now, let go of the clicker on your mouse, and there are all your numbers. (See Table 3-8.)

**TABLE 3-8**

| D3 | ▼ | = | =C3-B3 | |
|---|---|---|---|---|
| | A | B | C | D |
| 1 | Name | Last year | This year | Change |
| 2 | | | | |
| 3 | Dee Dale | $ 45,000 | $ 52,000 | $ 7,000 |
| 4 | Ed Powell | $ 25,000 | $ 30,000 | $ 5,000 |
| 5 | Jane Deed | $ 14,000 | $ 19,000 | $ 5,000 |
| 6 | Joe Smith | $ 30,000 | $ 39,000 | $ 9,000 |
| 7 | Julia Jones | $ 50,000 | $ 58,000 | $ 8,000 |
| 8 | Mark Forest | $ 15,000 | $ 21,000 | $ 6,000 |
| 9 | Mary Hill | $ 22,000 | $ 29,000 | $ 7,000 |
| 10 | Tom Brown | $ 40,000 | $ 47,000 | $ 7,000 |
| 11 | | | | |

What you have done is to tell the spreadsheet to do the same thing it did in D3 for the rest of the rows. As we said, the spreadsheet isn't going to copy $7,000 to every box in the D column. It's going to copy the formula of subtracting column B from the column C in each row. Always take a close look at the column after you have copied the formula. Some spreadsheets allow you to copy formulas easily, while others sometimes "guess" incorrectly at what formula you want to copy. Furthermore, if you copied the formula incorrectly, you will increase your error by however many rows to which you copy the formula.

So, the program subtracts B4 from C4, B5 from C5, and so on. Another way to copy the formula—if there are no blank rows—is to double-click once you see the narrow cross (as shown in Table 3-9, on p. 32). When you double-click, the formula will be copied and the numbers will appear until there is a blank row.

**TABLE 3-9**

|   | A | B | C | D |
|---|---|---|---|---|
| 1 | Name | Last year | This year | Change |
| 2 |  |  |  |  |
| 3 | Dee Dale | $ 45,000 | $ 52,000 | $ 7,000 |
| 4 | Ed Powell | $ 25,000 | $ 30,000 |  |
| 5 | Jane Deed | $ 14,000 | $ 19,000 |  |
| 6 | Joe Smith | $ 30,000 | $ 39,000 |  |
| 7 | Julia Jones | $ 50,000 | $ 58,000 |  |
| 8 | Mark Forest | $ 15,000 | $ 21,000 |  |
| 9 | Mary Hill | $ 22,000 | $ 29,000 |  |
| 10 | Tom Brown | $ 40,000 | $ 47,000 |  |
| 11 |  |  |  |  |

## ■▤▤ PERCENTAGES

When you look at salary increases, the largest increase is not
necessarily the most important. After all, $5,000 added to
$60,000 doesn't have the same impact as $5,000 added to
$30,000. Often, you will want to know who got the highest per-
centage increase. This brings you to a bugaboo of many journalists: the percentage difference.

In the late 1990s, many journalists could discuss for days
how to do percentage difference. But calculating a percentage
difference is straightforward if you break it down into its com-
ponents. If one of the mayor's cronies is making $45,000 and
gets a raise to $52,000, the difference is $7,000. In this example, the percentage difference is the increase ($7,000) over the
original salary: $7,000/$45,000. Now, divide 7,000 by 45,000.
That gives you .15$\bar{5}$, or (rounding up) 16 percent.

If you were saying it instead of calculating it, you would say,
"Subtract the first column from the second column, and divide
the result by the amount in the the first column. In this case,
it's $52,000 minus $45,000; then $7,000 divided by $45,000."

How would this look in a spreadsheet? You go to your spreadsheet and find the difference: $7,000. That's in box D3. Where's the old salary? In box B3. So your formula is D3/B3, as shown in Table 3-10.

**TABLE 3-10**

| | SUM | ▼ | ✕ ✓ = | =D3/B3 | |
|---|---|---|---|---|---|
| | A | B | C | D | E |
| 1 | Name | Last year | This year | Change | Percent |
| 2 | | | | | |
| 3 | Dee Dale | $ 45,000 | $ 52,000 | $ 7,000 | =D3/B3 |
| 4 | Ed Powell | $ 25,000 | $ 30,000 | $ 5,000 | |
| 5 | Jane Deed | $ 14,000 | $ 19,000 | $ 5,000 | |
| 6 | Joe Smith | $ 30,000 | $ 39,000 | $ 9,000 | |
| 7 | Julia Jones | $ 50,000 | $ 58,000 | $ 8,000 | |
| 8 | Mark Forest | $ 15,000 | $ 21,000 | $ 6,000 | |
| 9 | Mary Hill | $ 22,000 | $ 29,000 | $ 7,000 | |
| 10 | Tom Brown | $ 40,000 | $ 47,000 | $ 7,000 | |

Once again, you tip off the spreadsheet by typing the "=" sign in box E3, type "D3/B3," and hit "Enter." The result appears as shown in Table 3-11.

**TABLE 3-11**

| | A | B | C | D | E |
|---|---|---|---|---|---|
| 1 | Name | Last year | This year | Change | Percent |
| 2 | | | | | |
| 3 | Dee Dale | $ 45,000 | $ 52,000 | $ 7,000 | 0.155556 |
| 4 | Ed Powell | $ 25,000 | $ 30,000 | $ 5,000 | |
| 5 | Jane Deed | $ 14,000 | $ 19,000 | $ 5,000 | |
| 6 | Joe Smith | $ 30,000 | $ 39,000 | $ 9,000 | |
| 7 | Julia Jones | $ 50,000 | $ 58,000 | $ 8,000 | |
| 8 | Mark Forest | $ 15,000 | $ 21,000 | $ 6,000 | |
| 9 | Mary Hill | $ 22,000 | $ 29,000 | $ 7,000 | |
| 10 | Tom Brown | $ 40,000 | $ 47,000 | $ 7,000 | |

Again, to save time, you copy the formula using the narrow cross. Your result is shown in Table 3-12.

**TABLE 3-12**

| | A | B | C | D | E |
|---|---|---|---|---|---|
| 1 | Name | Last year | This year | Change | Percent |
| 2 | | | | | |
| 3 | Dee Dale | $ 45,000 | $ 52,000 | $ 7,000 | 0.155556 |
| 4 | Ed Powell | $ 25,000 | $ 30,000 | $ 5,000 | 0.2 |
| 5 | Jane Deed | $ 14,000 | $ 19,000 | $ 5,000 | 0.357143 |
| 6 | Joe Smith | $ 30,000 | $ 39,000 | $ 9,000 | 0.3 |
| 7 | Julia Jones | $ 50,000 | $ 58,000 | $ 8,000 | 0.16 |
| 8 | Mark Forest | $ 15,000 | $ 21,000 | $ 6,000 | 0.4 |
| 9 | Mary Hill | $ 22,000 | $ 29,000 | $ 7,000 | 0.318182 |
| 10 | Tom Brown | $ 40,000 | $ 47,000 | $ 7,000 | 0.175 |

There are many numbers to the right of the decimal, and it looks confusing. You would never print or broadcast percentages in this form. So, you highlight the column by clicking on the letter E above the top row, move the cursor onto the icon for the percent sign, and click on it, as shown in Table 3-13.

**TABLE 3-13**

| Arial | | ▼ 10 ▼ | **B** *I* <u>U</u> | ≡ ≡ ≡ 重 | $ % , | .0 .0 |
|---|---|---|---|---|---|---|
| | E1 | ▼ | = Percent | | | |

Percent Style

| | A | B | C | D | E |
|---|---|---|---|---|---|
| 1 | Name | Last year | This year | Change | Percent |
| 2 | | | | | |
| 3 | Dee Dale | $ 45,000 | $ 52,000 | $ 7,000 | 0.155556 |
| 4 | Ed Powell | $ 25,000 | $ 30,000 | $ 5,000 | 0.2 |
| 5 | Jane Deed | $ 14,000 | $ 19,000 | $ 5,000 | 0.357143 |
| 6 | Joe Smith | $ 30,000 | $ 39,000 | $ 9,000 | 0.3 |
| 7 | Julia Jones | $ 50,000 | $ 58,000 | $ 8,000 | 0.16 |
| 8 | Mark Forest | $ 15,000 | $ 21,000 | $ 6,000 | 0.4 |
| 9 | Mary Hill | $ 22,000 | $ 29,000 | $ 7,000 | 0.318182 |
| 10 | Tom Brown | $ 40,000 | $ 47,000 | $ 7,000 | 0.175 |

The outcome in Table 3-14 is much easier to read.

**TABLE 3-14**

| | A | B | C | D | E |
|---|---|---|---|---|---|
| 1 | Name | Last year | This year | Change | Percent |
| 2 | | | | | |
| 3 | Dee Dale | $ 45,000 | $ 52,000 | $ 7,000 | 16% |
| 4 | Ed Powell | $ 25,000 | $ 30,000 | $ 5,000 | 20% |
| 5 | Jane Deed | $ 14,000 | $ 19,000 | $ 5,000 | 36% |
| 6 | Joe Smith | $ 30,000 | $ 39,000 | $ 9,000 | 30% |
| 7 | Julia Jones | $ 50,000 | $ 58,000 | $ 8,000 | 16% |
| 8 | Mark Forest | $ 15,000 | $ 21,000 | $ 6,000 | 40% |
| 9 | Mary Hill | $ 22,000 | $ 29,000 | $ 7,000 | 32% |
| 10 | Tom Brown | $ 40,000 | $ 47,000 | $ 7,000 | 18% |

## FROM HORIZONTAL TO VERTICAL

By comparing rows, you have been doing calculations horizontally in the two-dimensional world of a spreadsheet. But you also can do vertical calculations. For the story on the mayor's cronies, you might want to know how much their salaries are costing taxpayers. For this, you need to total the numbers in the columns.

You move the cursor to the box in Table 3-15 in which you want the total to appear. (By the way, the individual boxes in a spreadsheet are called *cells*.)

**TABLE 3-15**

| SUM | ▼ | X ✓ = | =SUM(B3:B10) | | |
|---|---|---|---|---|---|
| | A | B | C | D | E |
| 1 | Name | Last year | This year | Change | Percent |
| 2 | | | | | |
| 3 | Dee Dale | $ 45,000 | $ 52,000 | $ 7,000 | 16% |
| 4 | Ed Powell | $ 25,000 | $ 30,000 | $ 5,000 | 20% |
| 5 | Jane Deed | $ 14,000 | $ 19,000 | $ 5,000 | 36% |
| 6 | Joe Smith | $ 30,000 | $ 39,000 | $ 9,000 | 30% |
| 7 | Julia Jones | $ 50,000 | $ 58,000 | $ 8,000 | 16% |
| 8 | Mark Forest | $ 15,000 | $ 21,000 | $ 6,000 | 40% |
| 9 | Mary Hill | $ 22,000 | $ 29,000 | $ 7,000 | 32% |
| 10 | Tom Brown | $ 40,000 | $ 47,000 | $ 7,000 | 18% |
| 11 | | | | | |
| 12 | Total | =SUM(B3:B10) | | | |
| 13 | | | | | |

You type the "=" again, then the word "SUM," and then the range of cells you want to total. In this case, the numbers start at B3 and end at B10. So, you type "=SUM(B3:B10)" as shown in Table 3-15 (p. 35), putting a colon between the beginning location and the ending location.

When you hit "Enter," the total appears as in Table 3-16.

**TABLE 3-16**

|   | A | B | C | D | E |
|---|---|---|---|---|---|
| 1 | Name | Last year | This year | Change | Percent |
| 2 |  |  |  |  |  |
| 3 | Dee Dale | $ 45,000 | $ 52,000 | $ 7,000 | 16% |
| 4 | Ed Powell | $ 25,000 | $ 30,000 | $ 5,000 | 20% |
| 5 | Jane Deed | $ 14,000 | $ 19,000 | $ 5,000 | 36% |
| 6 | Joe Smith | $ 30,000 | $ 39,000 | $ 9,000 | 30% |
| 7 | Julia Jones | $ 50,000 | $ 58,000 | $ 8,000 | 16% |
| 8 | Mark Forest | $ 15,000 | $ 21,000 | $ 6,000 | 40% |
| 9 | Mary Hill | $ 22,000 | $ 29,000 | $ 7,000 | 32% |
| 10 | Tom Brown | $ 40,000 | $ 47,000 | $ 7,000 | 18% |
| 11 |  |  |  |  |  |
| 12 | Total | $ 241,000 |  |  |  |

Rather than repeating the formula for each column, do what you did when calculating differences in rows: using the narrow cross, copy the formula horizontally, as shown in Table 3-17.

**TABLE 3-17**

| B12 | ▼ | **=** | =SUM(B3:B10) |  |  |
|---|---|---|---|---|---|
|   | A | B | C | D | E |
| 1 | Name | Last year | This year | Change | Percent |
| 2 |  |  |  |  |  |
| 3 | Dee Dale | $ 45,000 | $ 52,000 | $ 7,000 | 16% |
| 4 | Ed Powell | $ 25,000 | $ 30,000 | $ 5,000 | 20% |
| 5 | Jane Deed | $ 14,000 | $ 19,000 | $ 5,000 | 36% |
| 6 | Joe Smith | $ 30,000 | $ 39,000 | $ 9,000 | 30% |
| 7 | Julia Jones | $ 50,000 | $ 58,000 | $ 8,000 | 16% |
| 8 | Mark Forest | $ 15,000 | $ 21,000 | $ 6,000 | 40% |
| 9 | Mary Hill | $ 22,000 | $ 29,000 | $ 7,000 | 32% |
| 10 | Tom Brown | $ 40,000 | $ 47,000 | $ 7,000 | 18% |
| 11 |  |  |  |  |  |
| 12 | Total | $ 241,000 |  |  |  |
| 13 |  |  |  |  |  |

Let go of the mouse, and the results appear as shown in Table 3-18.

**TABLE 3-18**

| | D12 ▼ | | **=** =SUM(D3:D10) | | |
|---|---|---|---|---|---|
| | A | B | C | **D** | E |
| **1** | Name | Last year | This year | Change | Percent |
| **2** | | | | | |
| **3** | Dee Dale | $  45,000 | $  52,000 | $  7,000 | 16% |
| **4** | Ed Powell | $  25,000 | $  30,000 | $  5,000 | 20% |
| **5** | Jane Deed | $  14,000 | $  19,000 | $  5,000 | 36% |
| **6** | Joe Smith | $  30,000 | $  39,000 | $  9,000 | 30% |
| **7** | Julia Jones | $  50,000 | $  58,000 | $  8,000 | 16% |
| **8** | Mark Forest | $  15,000 | $  21,000 | $  6,000 | 40% |
| **9** | Mary Hill | $  22,000 | $  29,000 | $  7,000 | 32% |
| **10** | Tom Brown | $  40,000 | $  47,000 | $  7,000 | 18% |
| **11** | | | | | |
| **12** | Total | $  241,000 | $  295,000 | $ 54,000 | |
| **13** | | | | | |

You might also want to determine how the average increase for the mayor's cronies compares to the average 5 percent increase for all employees. There are two ways of doing this. To compare the average percentage increase for the mayor's cronies, giving equal weight to each employee regardless of salary, you would average the percentages in column E and get 26 percent. (You'll do an average of a column later in this chapter.)

But if you wanted to calculate the percentage increase in the total amount of money paid to the cronies, you would calculate the difference in the rows. To do that, you would not average the percentages. You would calculate the percentage difference between the totals (C12 and B12) by subtracting B12 from C12. The answer would appear in D12. Then, you would divide D12 by B12. The result, shown in Table 3-19 (p. 38), would be approximately 22 percent, or more than four times that of all employees.

**TABLE 3-19**

| | E12 | ▾ | ■ | =D12/B12 | |
|---|---|---|---|---|---|
| | A | B | C | D | E |
| 1 | Name | Last year | This year | Change | Percent |
| 2 | | | | | |
| 3 | Dee Dale | $  45,000 | $  52,000 | $  7,000 | 16% |
| 4 | Ed Powell | $  25,000 | $  30,000 | $  5,000 | 20% |
| 5 | Jane Deed | $  14,000 | $  19,000 | $  5,000 | 36% |
| 6 | Joe Smith | $  30,000 | $  39,000 | $  9,000 | 30% |
| 7 | Julia Jones | $  50,000 | $  58,000 | $  8,000 | 16% |
| 8 | Mark Forest | $  15,000 | $  21,000 | $  6,000 | 40% |
| 9 | Mary Hill | $  22,000 | $  29,000 | $  7,000 | 32% |
| 10 | Tom Brown | $  40,000 | $  47,000 | $  7,000 | 18% |
| 11 | | | | | |
| 12 | Total | $  241,000 | $  295,000 | $ 54,000 | 22% |

## ■▬ COMPARING THE PARTS TO THE SUM

You might also want to find out who got the biggest chunk of money out of the salary increases. If this were a city budget, you might want to see which department received the largest portion of the budget. In either case, you want to compare the individual raise for each person with the total amount of raises. Thus, you want to compare D3 with D12, D4 with D12, and so on.

However, a spreadsheet is used to moving down a row after each calculation. Without some hint of what you want to do, the spreadsheet will compare D3 with D12 and then D4 with D13, which would be nonsense. Thus, we need to "anchor" D12.

Fortunately, spreadsheets give us an easy way to accomplish this. As shown in Table 3-20, we anchor D12 by putting a dollar sign ("$") before the letter and a "$" before the number: "$D$12." The first dollar sign anchors the column, and the second dollar sign anchors the row. Now the spreadsheet knows to compare all the numbers in a column only with D12.

**TABLE 3-20**

| | SUM ▼ | X ✓ = | =D3/$D$12 | | | |
|---|---|---|---|---|---|---|
| | A | B | C | D | E | F |
| 1 | Name | Last year | This year | Change | Percent | Percent of Total |
| 2 | | | | | | |
| 3 | Dee Dale | $  45,000 | $  52,000 | $  7,000 | 16% | =D3/$D$12 |
| 4 | Ed Powell | $  25,000 | $  30,000 | $  5,000 | 20% | |
| 5 | Jane Deed | $  14,000 | $  19,000 | $  5,000 | 36% | |
| 6 | Joe Smith | $  30,000 | $  39,000 | $  9,000 | 30% | |
| 7 | Julia Jones | $  50,000 | $  58,000 | $  8,000 | 16% | |
| 8 | Mark Forest | $  15,000 | $  21,000 | $  6,000 | 40% | |
| 9 | Mary Hill | $  22,000 | $  29,000 | $  7,000 | 32% | |
| 10 | Tom Brown | $  40,000 | $  47,000 | $  7,000 | 18% | |
| 11 | | | | | | |
| 12 | Total | $  241,000 | $  295,000 | $ 54,000 | 22% | |

Tap the "Enter" key, and in Table 3-21 you obtain a new percentage of the total.

**TABLE 3-21**

| | A | B | C | D | E | F |
|---|---|---|---|---|---|---|
| 1 | Name | Last year | This year | Change | Percent | Percent of Total |
| 2 | | | | | | |
| 3 | Dee Dale | $  45,000 | $  52,000 | $  7,000 | 16% | 0.12962963 |
| 4 | Ed Powell | $  25,000 | $  30,000 | $  5,000 | 20% | |
| 5 | Jane Deed | $  14,000 | $  19,000 | $  5,000 | 36% | ✥ |
| 6 | Joe Smith | $  30,000 | $  39,000 | $  9,000 | 30% | |
| 7 | Julia Jones | $  50,000 | $  58,000 | $  8,000 | 16% | |
| 8 | Mark Forest | $  15,000 | $  21,000 | $  6,000 | 40% | |
| 9 | Mary Hill | $  22,000 | $  29,000 | $  7,000 | 32% | |
| 10 | Tom Brown | $  40,000 | $  47,000 | $  7,000 | 18% | |
| 11 | | | | | | |
| 12 | Total | $  241,000 | $  295,000 | $ 54,000 | 22% | |

Again, copy the formula. Then click the percentage icon. Table 3-22 (p. 40) shows the result.

**TABLE 3-22**

| F6 | ▼ | **=** | =D6/$D$12 | | | |
|---|---|---|---|---|---|---|
| | A | B | C | D | E | F |
| 1 | Name | Last year | This year | Change | Percent | Percent of Total |
| 2 | | | | | | |
| 3 | Dee Dale | $  45,000 | $  52,000 | $  7,000 | 16% | 13% |
| 4 | Ed Powell | $  25,000 | $  30,000 | $  5,000 | 20% | 9% |
| 5 | Jane Deed | $  14,000 | $  19,000 | $  5,000 | 36% | 9% |
| 6 | Joe Smith | $  30,000 | $  39,000 | $  9,000 | 30% | 17% |
| 7 | Julia Jones | $  50,000 | $  58,000 | $  8,000 | 16% | 15% |
| 8 | Mark Forest | $  15,000 | $  21,000 | $  6,000 | 40% | 11% |
| 9 | Mary Hill | $  22,000 | $  29,000 | $  7,000 | 32% | 13% |
| 10 | Tom Brown | $  40,000 | $  47,000 | $  7,000 | 18% | 13% |
| 11 | | | | | | |
| 12 | Total | $ 241,000 | $ 295,000 | $ 54,000 | 22% | |

From this calculation, you see that Joe Smith got the biggest chunk—17 percent—of the raises.

## ■▦ SORTING THE RESULTS

Journalists generally want to rank (or sort) information. If you were ranking information without a large spreadsheet, you'd have to go through hundreds of numbers to search for the highest percentage. Instead, a spreadsheet allows you to sort the information rapidly. This brings us to another bugaboo.

When you sort a spreadsheet, you need to keep all the information in each row together. But spreadsheets make sorting so easy that journalists often rush past this important point.

You must outline the entire area to be sorted. All rows of numbers should be highlighted. Many older versions of spreadsheets allowed you to sort one column of information without moving the rest of the row. That meant the percentages were suddenly scrambled and matched against the wrong information. In our current program, you outline the entire area, leaving out the titles of the columns and the totals, as shown in Table 3-23.

**TABLE 3-23**

| | A3 ▼ | | = | Dee Dale | | |
|---|---|---|---|---|---|---|
| | A | B | C | D | E | F |
| 1 | Name | Last year | This year | Change | Percent | Percent of Total |
| 2 | | | | | | |
| 3 | Dee Dale | $ 45,000 | $ 52,000 | $ 7,000 | 16% | 13% |
| 4 | Ed Powell | $ 25,000 | $ 30,000 | $ 5,000 | 20% | 9% |
| 5 | Jane Deed | $ 14,000 | $ 19,000 | $ 5,000 | 36% | 9% |
| 6 | Joe Smith | $ 30,000 | $ 39,000 | $ 9,000 | 30% | 17% |
| 7 | Julia Jones | $ 50,000 | $ 58,000 | $ 8,000 | 16% | 15% |
| 8 | Mark Forest | $ 15,000 | $ 21,000 | $ 6,000 | 40% | 11% |
| 9 | Mary Hill | $ 22,000 | $ 29,000 | $ 7,000 | 32% | 13% |
| 10 | Tom Brown | $ 40,000 | $ 47,000 | $ 7,000 | 18% | 13% |
| 11 | | | | | | |
| 12 | Total | $ 241,000 | $ 295,000 | $ 54,000 | 22% | |

You then decide to go to the "Sort" command under "Data" in the menu shown in Table 3-24.

**TABLE 3-24**

Clicking on "Sort" brings up the next screen, which gives you the opportunity to choose which column to sort by and in what order. Lowest to highest is called "ascending," and highest to lowest is called "descending." As shown in Table 3-25, you choose "Column E" and "Descending."

**TABLE 3-25**

Now click "OK." In Table 3-26, you see that Mark Forest received the highest percentage raise, 40 percent.

**TABLE 3-26**

| | A | B | C | D | E | F |
|---|---|---|---|---|---|---|
| | | | = | =D3/B3 | | |
| | Name | Last year | This year | Change | Percent | Percent of Total |
| 1 | Name | Last year | This year | Change | Percent | Percent of Total |
| 2 | | | | | | |
| 3 | Mark Forest | $ 15,000 | $ 21,000 | $ 6,000 | 40% | 11% |
| 4 | Jane Deed | $ 14,000 | $ 19,000 | $ 5,000 | 36% | 9% |
| 5 | Mary Hill | $ 22,000 | $ 29,000 | $ 7,000 | 32% | 13% |
| 6 | Joe Smith | $ 30,000 | $ 39,000 | $ 9,000 | 30% | 17% |
| 7 | Ed Powell | $ 25,000 | $ 30,000 | $ 5,000 | 20% | 9% |
| 8 | Tom Brown | $ 40,000 | $ 47,000 | $ 7,000 | 18% | 13% |
| 9 | Julia Jones | $ 50,000 | $ 58,000 | $ 8,000 | 16% | 15% |
| 10 | Dee Dale | $ 45,000 | $ 52,000 | $ 7,000 | 16% | 13% |
| 11 | | | | | | |
| 12 | Total | $ 241,000 | $ 295,000 | $ 54,000 | 22% | |

## ▰▰▰ PER CAPITA AND RATES

There is another type of comparison that is handy for journalists: a per capita figure. If you were to look at FBI statistics on murder in cities with a population larger than 100,000, it would not surprise you that New York City leads with 983 murders (see Table 3-27). After all, New York has the largest population, with 7,339,594 people. (This sample uses 1996 data.)

**TABLE 3-27**

| | A | B | C | D |
|---|---|---|---|---|
| | **Murder96** | | | |
| 1 | CITY | STATE | MURDERS | POPULATION |
| 2 | New York | NY | 983 | 7,339,594 |
| 3 | Chicago | IL | 789 | 2,754,118 |
| 4 | Los Angeles | CA | 711 | 3,498,139 |
| 5 | Detroit | MI | 428 | 1,002,299 |
| 6 | Washington | D.C. | 397 | 543,000 |
| 7 | New Orleans | LA | 351 | 488,300 |
| 8 | Baltimore | MD | 330 | 716,446 |
| 9 | Houston | TX | 261 | 1,772,143 |
| 10 | Dallas | TX | 217 | 1,060,585 |
| 11 | Atlanta | GA | 196 | 413,123 |
| 12 | Phoenix | AZ | 186 | 1,139,793 |

But would the number of murders indicate how dangerous New York is when compared to other cities? No. One way to get a good idea is to use a per capita figure. Now that you know formulas, you know how easy it is to put a calculation into a spreadsheet.

In Table 3-28, you divide the number of murders in New York (C2) by the city's population (D2). You then multiply that number by 100,000 to get the murder rate per 100,000 persons.

**TABLE 3-28**

| | A | B | C | D | E |
|---|---|---|---|---|---|
| 1 | CITY | STATE | MURDERS | POPULATION | PER CAPITA |
| 2 | New York | NY | 983 | 7,339,594 | =C2/D2*100000 |
| 3 | Chicago | IL | 789 | 2,754,118 | |
| 4 | Los Angeles | CA | 711 | 3,498,139 | |
| 5 | Detroit | MI | 428 | 1,002,299 | |
| 6 | Washington | D.C. | 397 | 543,000 | |
| 7 | New Orleans | LA | 351 | 488,300 | |
| 8 | Baltimore | MD | 330 | 716,446 | |
| 9 | Houston | TX | 261 | 1,772,143 | |
| 10 | Dallas | TX | 217 | 1,060,585 | |
| 11 | Atlanta | GA | 196 | 413,123 | |
| 12 | Phoenix | AZ | 186 | 1,139,793 | |

If you didn't multiply by 100,000, you would get a per capita (or per person) figure with several decimal places: .0001339. This number would not be very meaningful to a reader or viewer of the news. By multiplying by 100,000, you get a rate of 13.39 murders per 100,000 people, as shown in Table 3-29.

**TABLE 3-29**

| | A | B | C | D | E |
|---|---|---|---|---|---|
| 1 | CITY | STATE | MURDERS | POPULATION | PER CAPITA |
| 2 | New York | NY | 983 | 7,339,594 | 13.39 |
| 3 | Chicago | IL | 789 | 2,754,118 | |
| 4 | Los Angeles | CA | 711 | 3,498,139 | |
| 5 | Detroit | MI | 428 | 1,002,299 | |
| 6 | Washington | D.C. | 397 | 543,000 | |
| 7 | New Orleans | LA | 351 | 488,300 | |
| 8 | Baltimore | MD | 330 | 716,446 | |

Next, to obtain a rate for each city, copy the formula down the column (see Table 3-30). (Also, note we have changed "per capita" to "rate.")

**TABLE 3-30**

| | A | B | C | D | E |
|---|---|---|---|---|---|
| 1 | CITY | STATE | MURDERS | POPULATION | RATE |
| 2 | New York | NY | 983 | 7,339,594 | 13.39 |
| 3 | Chicago | IL | 789 | 2,754,118 | 28.65 |
| 4 | Los Angeles | CA | 711 | 3,498,139 | 20.33 |
| 5 | Detroit | MI | 428 | 1,002,299 | 42.70 |
| 6 | Washington | D.C. | 397 | 543,000 | 73.11 |
| 7 | New Orleans | LA | 351 | 488,300 | 71.88 |
| 8 | Baltimore | MD | 330 | 716,446 | 46.06 |

Then sort the information in descending order by column E. You find, as shown in Table 3-31, that Gary, Indiana, has the most murders per 100,000 people. New York City doesn't even make the top ten.

**TABLE 3-31**

| | A | B | C | D | E |
|---|---|---|---|---|---|
| 1 | CITY | STATE | MURDERS | POPULATION | RATE |
| 2 | Gary | IN | 104 | 116,024 | 89.64 |
| 3 | Washington | D.C. | 397 | 543,000 | 73.11 |
| 4 | New Orleans | LA | 351 | 488,300 | 71.88 |
| 5 | Richmond | VA | 112 | 204,881 | 54.67 |
| 6 | Atlanta | GA | 196 | 413,123 | 47.44 |
| 7 | Baltimore | MD | 330 | 716,446 | 46.06 |
| 8 | Saint Louis | MO | 166 | 374,041 | 44.38 |
| 9 | Detroit | MI | 428 | 1,002,299 | 42.70 |
| 10 | Birmingham | AL | 113 | 272,169 | 41.52 |

# ■▬ CHARTS AND GRAPHS

There is one last chore that can make all the difference in spreadsheets: displaying the results using graphics. Spreadsheets permit you to quickly place information into bar charts, pie charts, or other kinds of charts. In this example, the different percentage increases in salaries might go into a bar chart.

You want to make a chart that shows which employee received the highest percentage. First, highlight the "Name" column. Then, holding down the "Control" key, move the cursor to the "Percent" (of raises) column, and highlight that column.

Then, click on the "chart wizard" icon. A chart wizard helps you select the kind of chart you want to create. The arrow in Table 3-32 points to the icon.

**TABLE 3-32**

File  Edit  View  Insert  Format  Tools  Data  Window  Help

Arial    10    **B** *I* U    $ % ,    Chart Wizard

E3    =D3/B3

| | A | B | C | D | E | F | G |
|---|---|---|---|---|---|---|---|
| 1 | Name | Last year | This year | Change | Percent | Percent of Total | |
| 2 | | | | | | | |
| 3 | Mark Forest | $ 15,000 | $ 21,000 | $ 6,000 | 40% | 11% | |
| 4 | Jane Deed | $ 14,000 | $ 19,000 | $ 5,000 | 36% | 9% | |
| 5 | Mary Hill | $ 22,000 | $ 29,000 | $ 7,000 | 32% | 13% | |
| 6 | Joe Smith | $ 30,000 | $ 39,000 | $ 9,000 | 30% | 17% | |
| 7 | Ed Powell | $ 25,000 | $ 30,000 | $ 5,000 | 20% | 9% | |
| 8 | Tom Brown | $ 40,000 | $ 47,000 | $ 7,000 | 18% | 13% | |
| 9 | Julia Jones | $ 50,000 | $ 58,000 | $ 8,000 | 16% | 15% | |
| 10 | Dee Dale | $ 45,000 | $ 52,000 | $ 7,000 | 16% | 13% | |
| 11 | | | | | | | |
| 12 | Total | $ 241,000 | $ 295,000 | $ 54,000 | 22% | | |
| 13 | | | | | | | |

After you click on the icon, the wizard leads you through a series of steps in which you choose the kind of chart you want to create. In Table 3-33, the wizard has highlighted the "Column" chart for you.

**TABLE 3-33**

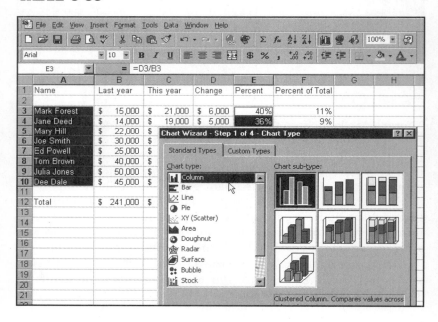

Follow the steps the wizard lays out for you, and eventually you will see a chart that displays your information, as in Table 3-34. Note that such charts can be enlarged and moved around.

**TABLE 3-34**

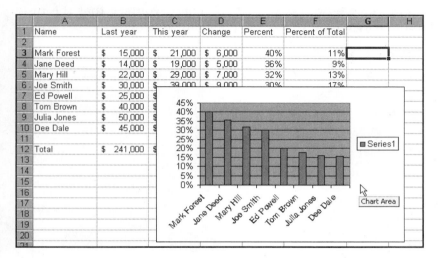

| | A | B | C | D | E | F | G | H |
|---|---|---|---|---|---|---|---|---|
| 1 | Name | Last year | This year | Change | Percent | Percent of Total | | |
| 2 | | | | | | | | |
| 3 | Mark Forest | $ 15,000 | $ 21,000 | $ 6,000 | 40% | 11% | | |
| 4 | Jane Deed | $ 14,000 | $ 19,000 | $ 5,000 | 36% | 9% | | |
| 5 | Mary Hill | $ 22,000 | $ 29,000 | $ 7,000 | 32% | 13% | | |
| 6 | Joe Smith | $ 30,000 | $ 39,000 | $ 9,000 | 30% | 17% | | |
| 7 | Ed Powell | $ 25,000 | | | | | | |
| 8 | Tom Brown | $ 40,000 | | | | | | |
| 9 | Julia Jones | $ 50,000 | | | | | | |
| 10 | Dee Dale | $ 45,000 | | | | | | |
| 11 | | | | | | | | |
| 12 | Total | $ 241,000 | | | | | | |
| 13 | | | | | | | | |

You also can easily represent a budget with a pie chart or measure increases in crime with a bar chart. Sometimes, using a chart helps you see the results of your work more clearly. For example, residents of a city believe they are paying too much for sewer and water services. They claim that commercial businesses use more water and put a burden on the sewer system but don't pay their fair share. You obtain the budget figures for revenue from the water and sewer division and put them on a spreadsheet, as shown in Table 3-35.

**TABLE 3-35**

| B10 | ▼ | = | =SUM(B4:B8) |
|---|---|---|---|

| | A | B |
|---|---|---|
| 1 | | |
| 2 | Water and Sewer Division | 1998-1999 |
| 3 | | |
| 4 | Residential water fees | $ 13,235,122 |
| 5 | Residential sewer fees | $ 6,544,344 |
| 6 | Commercial water fees | $ 10,882,021 |
| 7 | Commercial sewer fees | $ 2,343,123 |
| 8 | Investment interest | $ 555,456 |
| 9 | | |
| 10 | Total | $ 33,560,066 |

Then you can quickly format the revenues into a pie chart, as in Table 3-36. Looking at the chart, you see that the residents may have a legitimate complaint.

**TABLE 3-36**

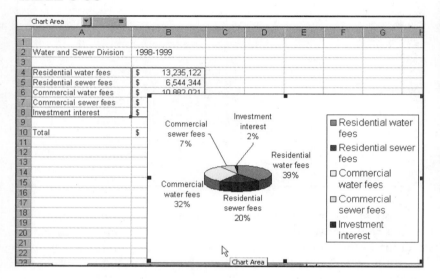

As you can see, spreadsheets can save journalists time, help them do quick analysis, and provide vivid graphics that illuminate the results.

## ▣▤ Chapter Summary

❏ Spreadsheets can help you do calculations faster and more easily.

❏ Spreadsheets use letters to identify columns and numbers to identify rows.

❏ For calculations, spreadsheets allow you to use column letters and row numbers to create formulas.

❏ Percentage difference often provides a fairer comparison than do raw numbers.

SPREADSHEETS **49**

- [ ] When you are comparing the parts of a calculation with the sum, be sure to "anchor" the sum.
- [ ] When you sort data, make sure to highlight the entire range of numbers that you want to sort.
- [ ] Rates are often fairer than plain numbers.
- [ ] Remember to use graphs and charts.

## ▪▦ SUGGESTED TASKS

- [ ] Obtain a list of names and salaries from your city, county, or state in electronic form or in hard copy.
- [ ] Obtain a part of a city, county, or state budget in electronic form or in hard copy. Make sure you get two years' worth.
- [ ] Put one or both data sets into a worksheet in a spreadsheet program.
- [ ] Sort the data in descending order using the salary. Then sort the data in descending order using the amount of each budget.
- [ ] Calculate the difference in the budget years. Calculate the percentage difference.

- [ ] Obtain crime statistics for the past three years from the FBI for your state.
- [ ] Find the population of your state and its major cities. *Hint:* The Census Bureau's Web site at <http://www.census.gov> has population figures.
- [ ] Place the number of crimes in a worksheet. Place the population figures in the same worksheet.
- [ ] Calculate the number of crimes per 100,000 persons. Calculate the percentage changes over three years. Chart those changes.

*Hint:* The National Institute for Computer-Assisted Reporting has some of these data.

# DATABASE MANAGERS: GOING FROM THE ROLODEX TO MATCHMAKING

> DEAD OR ALIVE, CITY'S INELIGIBLE VOTERS
> NUMBER IN THE THOUSANDS
>
> A man named Admiral Wherry, an army veteran who owned a barbecue pit and tire repair shop in East St. Louis, died more than two years ago.
>
> But that didn't stop him from voting in the Illinois Democratic primary on March 20.

This is how the *St. Louis Post-Dispatch* began its story about possible voter fraud in East St. Louis.[1] By using a database manager and comparing the addresses of registered voters with addresses of vacant lots, reporters George Landau and Tim Novak got the lead for a story. Then they matched the voters' list to a list of death certificates. This gave them a story on dead voters, which has also been done at such newspapers as the *Boston Herald,* the *Asbury Park Press,* and the *Chicago Sun Times.*

Unlike a spreadsheet, a database manager can examine hundreds of thousands of records in minutes, organize them into similar groups, and compare records in one database with records in another database. Many reporters use database man-

---

[1] Shesgreen, D. The Data Entry Ordeal. *Uplink* (March 1993), p. 4.

agers to do what they call the "heavy lifting" of data—that is, the searching and summarizing of large databases.

Although the dead voter story has proven popular, many journalists start with a simpler project: converting campaign records from paper to computer. For years, journalists have kept tabs on campaign contributions to politicians. Some have kept lists, some have kept index cards, some have kept the information in their heads. It can take a lot of time to retrieve that information and even more time to perform calculations to determine which politician is getting the most contributions and which donor is giving the most money.

It is ironic that many journalists have persisted in using paper when (1) the politicians' campaign managers use electronic databases, and (2) social scientists and nonprofit watchdog institutes use electronic databases to evaluate and criticize the donations. It's a good example of journalists standing in the breakdown lane of the information superhighway and watching others zoom by. One journalist for the Associated Press decided in the early 1990s that he had had enough and helped develop a campaign finance database in Pennsylvania. "I built my own database with index cards," David Morris said. "Then I decided it was time to move into the 20th century."

If you want to learn how to use database managers in a fairly quick and practical way, tracking political contributions is one of the best ways to begin. The Federal Election Commission in Washington, D.C., has a database of contributions to candidates for Congress and the presidency that you can obtain online or on diskette or computer tape. (Computer tapes and how to handle them are explained in Chapter 8.)

Some states have databases on state candidates, and many news organizations create their own electronic databases of local campaign contributions. As a result, there's a good selection of stories to examine to see how data can be turned into a story. (Not many editors oppose doing stories on this subject because most consider the monitoring of political contributions, and how contributions influence governmental actions, as required public service.)

In addition to serving as an instant resource for daily stories, a campaign finance database can be used for longer analytical stories. After the election, a reporter can do a story on how much money the winner received and who donated it. Then, after the winner takes office and begins to award no-bid contracts, the reporter can quickly determine whether the recipients had donated to the winner and, if so, how much they had contributed. A typical headline might read "Mayor's Supporters Get Lucrative Contracts."

One reason that campaign contributions are good fodder for learning database managers is that initially only three columns of information have to be considered (see Table 4-1).

| TABLE 4-1 | | |
|-----------|---|---|
| *Candidate* | *Contribution* | *Donor* |

Looking back at the 1996 presidential election, we might enter names and amounts under these columns, as shown in Table 4-2 (all donor names in this chapter are fictional).

| TABLE 4-2 | | |
|-----------|---|---|
| *Candidate* | *Contribution* | *Donor* |
| Dole, Robert | 1500 | Jesse Smith |
| Clinton, Bill | 2000 | John Hall |

Now, after having learned spreadsheets, you might question why you need to learn another piece of software. Well, let's assume your list is much longer than the one in Table 4-2 and contains thousands of contributions. In a spreadsheet, the names might appear as they do in Table 4-3.

**TABLE 4-3**

| A1 | ▼ | = | Candidate | |
|----|---|---|-----------|---|
| | A | B | C | |
| 1 | Candidate | Contribution | Donor | |
| 2 | Dole, Robert | 1000 | Ethel Brown | |
| 3 | Dole, Robert | 2000 | Jerry Hobbs | |
| 4 | Clinton, Bill | 500 | Laurel Ax | |
| 5 | Clinton, Bill | 1500 | Joe Tibbs | |
| 6 | Dole, Robert | 1000 | Martha Eib | |

But it's not too different to put the names into a database manager, as shown in Table 4-4.

**TABLE 4-4**

| President Race 96 : Table | | |
|---|---|---|
| **Candidate** | **Contribution** | **Donor** |
| Dole, Robert | 1000 | Ethel Brown |
| Dole, Robert | 2000 | Jerry Hobbs |
| Clinton, Bill | 500 | Laurel Ax |
| Clinton, Bill | 1500 | Joe Tibbs |
| Dole, Robert | 1000 | Martha Eib |
| Dole, Robert | 500 | Jack Cartwright |
| Clinton, Bill | 1500 | George Dayton |
| Clinton, Bill | 2000 | Cary Young |
| Clinton, Bill | 1000 | Bill Smith |
| Clinton, Bill | 2000 | Jill Cartwright |

Note there are no longer letters and numbers to guide you. One difference between spreadsheets and database managers is that information in spreadsheets usually comes to you in some sort of order. In database managers, the information initially may be in random order because the software assumes you will constantly reorder the information.

A database manager is designed to help you look up names quickly. Even if there were 25,000 donors, you could find in seconds one donor's name or all the donors who gave to Bob Dole. You could sort the list alphabetically or by amounts. You could even total the amounts given to each candidate, as in Table 4-5.

**TABLE 4-5**

| Query1 : Select Query | |
|---|---|
| **Candidate** | **SumOfContrib** |
| Clinton, Bill | 11000 |
| Dole, Robert | 8000 |

Table 4-5 shows what some journalists call "summary data." It is a summary of many records. The table also illustrates the concept of "grouping." *Grouping* means lumping together all similar kinds of records. Journalists use it when they are going to count the number of records or sum up amounts.

For many journalists (including myself), grouping was a difficult concept at first. A few years ago, it occurred to me that when we use grouping in a database manager, we are playing cards with databases. So I started handing out playing cards when I taught.

In most card games, you are dealt a hand. You might count the number of cards in each suit, and sometimes you sum up the face value of the cards. Before you do that, however, you arrange the cards by grouping them into suits.

In a game of bridge, you are dealt 13 cards: king of hearts, queen of hearts, five of clubs, seven of hearts, five of hearts, ace of diamonds, jack of spades, four of diamonds, eight of spades, six of spades, ten of diamonds, two of hearts, and three of diamonds. You divide them into suits: hearts, diamonds, spades, and clubs. You count the cards. You have five hearts, four diamonds, three spades, and one club. You sum up the face values (face cards are worth 10 and aces 1) and find you have 34 points in hearts, 18 in diamonds, 24 in spades, and 5 in clubs. Table 4-6 represents your findings.

| TABLE 4-6 | | |
|---|---|---|
| *Suit* | *Count (Number)* | *Sum (Face Value)* |
| Hearts | 5 | 34 |
| Diamonds | 4 | 18 |
| Spades | 3 | 24 |
| Clubs | 1 | 5 |

A database manager will do exactly this kind of work for you. Of course, you don't need it for card games, but you do need it for political contribution games.

Let's go back to our example from the presidential election. If you want to find out the various totals for the candidates, then you have the equivalent of two suits: Clinton and Dole. The face value is the contribution.

We'll return to grouping later. For now, we'll explore the basic uses of a database manager. We'll use the database manager known as Microsoft Access—but remember, the concepts are present in all database managers.

## ■ ■■■ Selecting and Searching

The first strength of a database manager is that it allows you to search for particular information quickly. If we want to find a name, we tell the database manager that we want to look for all the information on that particular name.

First, we select the columns we want to use. The concept of "select" is part of our database manager. Often, a database might have 30 or so columns, or "fields," of information.

Selection of the fields is important because it clears away distractions. Furthermore, many journalists' analyses eventually involve only three or four fields. In Table 4-7, you need to select only two fields to see who gave how much to the presidential campaign.

**TABLE 4-7**

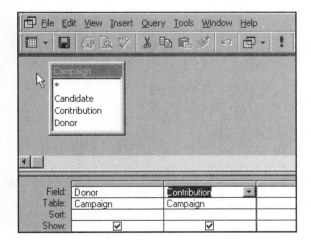

Note that "Donor" appears in one column and "Contribution" in the second. Underneath, you put a check mark in the "Show" box so that the information in the column will appear in the answer. (Another aspect of database managers is that you have to formulate your question and then "run" it. Journalists have likened a database manager to a bureaucrat because it requires you to fill out a form and then submit it for action.)

If we decide to run the query by hitting "!" in the toolbar at the top of the screen, we will get everything in those two columns, as shown in Table 4-8.

**TABLE 4-8**

| Donor | Contribution |
|---|---|
| Ethel Brown | 1000 |
| Jerry Hobbs | 2000 |
| Laurel Ax | 500 |
| Joe Tibbs | 1500 |
| Martha Eib | 1000 |
| Jack Cartwright | 500 |
| George Dayton | 1500 |
| Cary Young | 2000 |
| Bill Smith | 1000 |
| Jill Cartwright | 2000 |
| Dallas Thomas | 1000 |
| Douglas Knotts | 1000 |
| Jack Cartwright | 500 |

Record: 1 of 16

We have not lost any of the other information in the table but have simply selected two columns to show in our answer. If we don't save this result, it will simply disappear when we return to the original information.

## CRITERIA AND FILTERING

After looking at the fields, you might want to look only at contributors who gave more than $500. Move the cursor into the criteria box under "Contribution," and type "> 500" as shown in Table 4-9.

**TABLE 4-9**

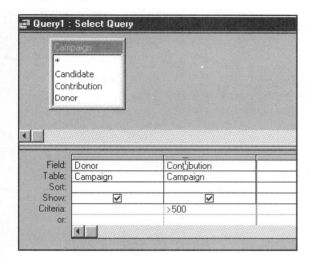

Run the query, and the answer appears as in Table 4-10.

**TABLE 4-10**

| Donor | Contribution |
|-------|--------------|
| Ethel Brown | 1000 |
| Jerry Hobbs | 2000 |
| Joe Tibbs | 1500 |
| Martha Eib | 1000 |
| George Dayton | 1500 |
| Cary Young | 2000 |
| Bill Smith | 1000 |
| Jill Cartwright | 2000 |
| Dallas Thomas | 1000 |
| Douglas Knotts | 1000 |
| Jack Cartwright | 1500 |
| Don Cartwright | 1500 |
| * | 0 |

Record: 1 of 12

## SORTING

If you want to sort the contributions from highest to lowest, you use the same principle as spreadsheets. Choose the column, and identify the sorting order as "Descending," as shown in Table 4-11.

**TABLE 4-11**

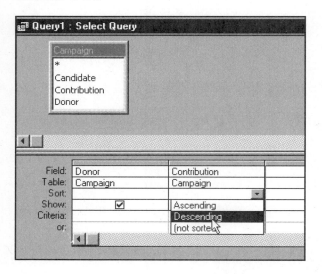

## CRITERIA AND WILDCARDS

Database managers allow you to single out one individual by using filters. The filters may be under "Criteria," or they may be in "where" statements, such as "where Donor = Cartwright." But database managers also have a powerful filtering function called "like." "Like" lets you choose a name by using only the first few letters of the name. Because data entry can be an error-prone endeavor, names are often spelled in several different ways in governmental databases. Using "like" is one way to get around the problem of misspelled entries.

As shown in Table 4-12, you can look for all donors named Cartwright by using "like" and a wildcard. In the Access data-

**TABLE 4-12**

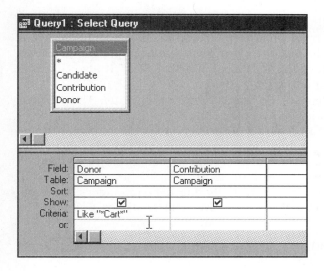

base manager, the wildcard is an asterisk (*). In other systems, it may be a percent sign (%) or two periods (. .). In any case, a wildcard in front of "Cart" stands for all the numbers or letters that might precede the letters "cart," and the asterisk after "Cart" stands for all the numbers or letters that might follow those four letters.

In Table 4-12, you wrote 'Like "*Cart*"'; Table 4-13 shows your result.

**TABLE 4-13**

| Donor | Contribution |
|---|---|
| Jack Cartwright | 500 |
| Jill Cartwright | 2000 |
| Matt McCarty | 1000 |
| Jack Cartwright | 500 |
| Jack Cartwright | 1500 |
| Ellen Cartwright | 500 |
| Don Cartwright | 1500 |

## ▋▇▇ BOOLEAN LOGIC: AND, OR, NOT

Another strength of database managers is that a search can incorporate two or more criteria. To do such a search, we use a logic that sounds like an alien from another planet—Boolean logic. Some modern librarians call it a "life skill." It also is a routine way of doing online searches.

Boolean logic uses the words *and, or,* and *not.* Those three little words are incredibly powerful.

You might want to search for everyone who gave more than $500 to Dole or Clinton. Boolean logic treats the search in this way: Give me the names of everyone who donated to Clinton or Dole and who gave more than $500.

Access and other user-friendly database managers are making it easy to do Boolean logic. In most searches online or in more sophisticated databases, you would write:

> where (candidate = "Dole" or candidate = "Clinton")
> and contribution > 500

You have to pay attention to your "or's" and "and's" and be very careful with "not's." If you are choosing items in the same field, don't write:

> where city = "New York" and city = "Los Angeles"

How can a person be in two places at once?

Also, as a general rule, if you are choosing items in the same field, put parentheses around them. For example, if you are looking for all the murderers among the criminals in New York City or Los Angeles, you would write:

> where city = ("New York" or "Los Angeles") and
> crime = "murderers"

If you write:

> where city = "New York" or city = "Los Angeles" and
> crime = "murderers"

you would probably get all the criminals in New York City and Los Angeles and all the murderers in the U.S.

"Not" is particularly handy when you want to exclude a set of information. If you are analyzing an election in Wisconsin and you wanted to look at only out-of-state contributors, you would use a "not." You would write a query that meant:

where state = not "Wisconsin"

## GROUPING

Once you have selected your fields, set your criteria, and then sorted, you still might want to know which candidate received the most money. This is where grouping is useful.

Your fields are Donor and Contribution. Because you are going to total the contributions for each candidate, you will group the contributions by candidate and you will sum the contributions. You always need to group by all fields that you are going to show but are not doing calculations on. See Table 4-14.

**TABLE 4-14**

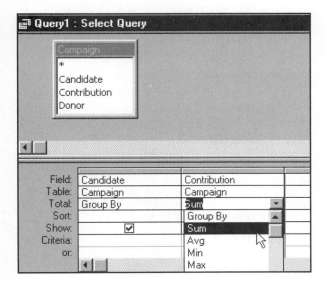

Your result will look like the example in Table 4-15 (p. 62). The total contributions will appear next to each candidate's name.

**TABLE 4-15**

| Query1 : Select Query | |
|---|---|
| **Candidate** | **SumOfContrib** |
| ▶ Clinton, Bill | 11000 |
| Dole, Robert | 8000 |

You might also want to know how many contributions each candidate received. The principle of grouping does not change. Now you are going to count the number of contributions by candidate, as shown in Table 4-16.

**TABLE 4-16**

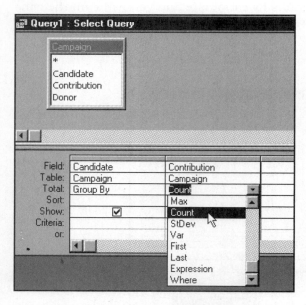

Your result this time will look like Table 4-17.

**TABLE 4-17**

| Query1 : Select Query | |
|---|---|
| **Candidate** | **CountOfContri** |
| ▶ Clinton, Bill | 9 |
| Dole, Robert | 7 |

Once you feel comfortable using these different queries, you can use a formula that has been the basis for many computer stories. With this formula, you obtain information, divide the information into groups, count or sum parts of the information by groups, and sort the results from highest to lowest. (In the midst of the query, you can filter in or filter out information with "where" statements.)

Once you know the formula, you can examine many different kinds of information. You could look at a prison population, divide it into races, and then count the number to find the percentage of minorities and whites in prison. You could then compare the percentages to the percentage of minorities and whites in the community.

You could look at blighted properties in your city, divide the information into neighborhoods, and then count the number of blighted properties in each neighborhood. You could take thousands of records of federal contracts in your state, divide the information by communities in which work is being done, sum the amounts of the contracts, and then get an idea of the economic importance of the contracts to those communities. You could look at records of toxic chemical emissions by manufacturers into the environment, divide the information by communities, sum the emissions by communities, and then find out which community has the most toxic releases.

Much of the information you collect can be examined in this way.

### ▧▤▤ Matchmaking

One of the most productive and imaginative uses of a database manager is matching information in one file to another.

Files that are intentionally linked are known as *relational databases*. Files are sometimes put together in this way because it helps organize information and save space.

Consider any job you've had. The company probably kept information about you in a relational database. In one file (or "table") is much of an employee's personal information, as shown in Table 4-18 on p. 64.

## TABLE 4-18

| Employee : Table | |
|---|---|
| **Field Name** | **Data Type** |
| ▶ Employee ID | Text |
| Last name | Text |
| First name | Text |
| Street | Text |
| Town | Text |

In another file is a list of the paychecks the employee received and the date on which the employee received them, as shown in Table 4-19.

## TABLE 4-19

| Employee pay : Table | |
|---|---|
| **Field Name** | **Data Type** |
| ▶ Employee ID | Text |
| Pay | Number |
| Date | Date/Time |

Note that each field has an Employee ID and that only an ID, not a name, appears in the salary table. The ID field is known as a *key field*. It's the field that links the two tables together, as shown in Table 4-20.

## TABLE 4-20

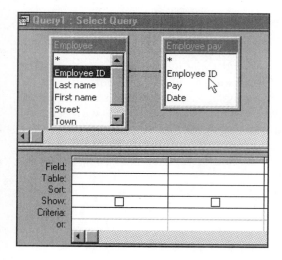

By linking the two tables, you can match each employee's name with his or her payroll information. This saves space because you don't have to type all the information about the employee each time you enter information about payroll. The tables also organize information efficiently into subjects.

What's the most universal key field in the United States? The Social Security number. With someone's Social Security number, you can link tables and tables of information together.

But how do you perform the link? You tell the program that when the ID number in a record in the employee table equals the ID number in the payroll table, then the information should be matched. In many database managers, this is much easier to do than it used to be. In Access, you can actually draw a line from one table to another by clicking on the Employee ID field in the Employee table and then dragging the cursor onto the ID in the Employee Pay table. In other database managers, the software automatically guesses the connection for you. In others, you write a "where" statement that says to link the two files together (for the example in Table 4-20 you might write in another database manager, "where employee.employee_id =employee_pay.employee_id").

Why should you care about an employee relational database? Well, many governmental databases are relational, especially if they contain employee information. You need to know what bureaucrats mean when they say a database is relational. You also need to know to ask what the key field is.

One of the more popular databases is produced by the Federal Election Commission (FEC). If you order data from the FEC, you will get a candidates table, a political action committee contribution table, an individual contributor table, and a political committee table. Those tables are linked by the ID numbers of committees and candidates.

To find information about a candidate, you would go to the candidates table. In that table, you would find ID numbers for the committees set up by the candidate to receive contributions. To find information about the committees, you would link the candidates table to the political committee table using the ID numbers. To determine which individuals contributed to the candidate, you would link the committee table to the individual contributor table using the committee ID that is present in both tables. It's like building bridges between islands of information.

## ENTERPRISING MATCHMAKING

Sometimes, the government uses enterprising matchmaking to ferret out criminals. Some states match labor department records with unemployment records to find people who are collecting unemployment while working at a job. You can guess what the key field is: the Social Security number.

Journalists can do extraordinary work by linking databases not originally intended to be linked. They can cross the borders between agencies, professions, and fiefdoms. But journalists don't always have the Social Security number. Therefore, they must be creative. When a relationship is not intended, they have to come up with one or more key fields. As we have seen, journalists seeking dead voters have linked street addresses or names of voters with names on death certificates. Several reporters have found criminals working as schoolteachers despite laws that prohibit felons—in particular, child molesters—from being hired. In general, such discoveries have been made by linking court or prison records to employee records by matching first name to first name, last name to last name, and date of birth to date of birth.

Table 4-21, for example, lists some fictional teachers.

**TABLE 4-21**

| Lastname | Firstname | Date of Birth | Date of Hire | School |
|----------|-----------|---------------|--------------|--------|
| Smith | Joseph | 11/1/65 | 1/10/90 | Nixon |
| Barry | Donald | 10/12/55 | 5/4/90 | Kennedy |
| Neff | Arnold | 4/2/59 | 8/3/91 | Jefferson |
| Harwood | Mary | 3/14/69 | 8/3/91 | Jefferson |
| Atwater | Gerald | 2/1/53 | 9/5/91 | Madison |

Table 4-22 lists criminals (also fictional).

**TABLE 4-22**

| Criminal : Table | | | | |
|---|---|---|---|---|
| **Lastname** | **Firstname** | **Date of Birth** | **Charge** | **Sentence** |
| Barry | Donald | 10/12/55 | Child molest | |
| Smith | Walter | 2/14/57 | Child molest | |
| Walker | Edward | 5/10/61 | Child molest | |
| Nadell | Samuel | 12/4/62 | Rape | |
| Harwood | Mary | 3/14/69 | Illegal gun | |

You would match them by looking at both tables at once and linking them by several fields, as shown in Table 4-23.

**TABLE 4-23**

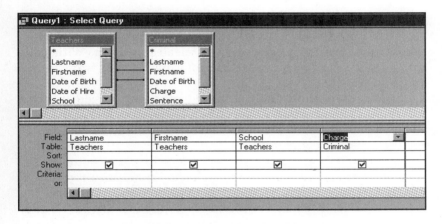

The result would look like Table 4-24.

**TABLE 4-24**

| Query1 : Select Query | | | |
|---|---|---|---|
| **Lastname** | **Firstname** | **School** | **Charge** |
| Barry | Donald | Kennedy | Child molest |
| Harwood | Mary | Jefferson | Illegal gun |

If you have a list of foster parents in your state and a list of criminal records, a good number of matches (or "hits") would lead to good public service journalism. The *Charlotte Observer* in North Carolina produced such a story. In Massachusetts, Brad Goldstein, formerly of the *Lawrence Eagle Tribune* and recently of the *St. Petersburg Times,* found welfare recipients in jail; he matched the names of recipients with a list of prison inmates. At the *Miami Herald,* Steve Doig matched building inspection records after Hurricane Andrew with wind velocities in the area. If the velocity was low and the damage was high, it indicated there probably was a problem with construction standards.

Matchmaking possibilities are limited only by the imagination of the journalist and the validity of the comparison.

## ■▨▨▨ Building Your Own Database

You are not restricted to using others' databases. A database manager permits you to build your own. In fact, often the information you want does not exist in electronic form. With your own database, you can enter the information you want in the way you want it.

Many reporters initially build a database to keep track of information about political contributors. Such a database might include the contributor's name, address, amount given, recipient, and date of contribution.

In a database manager, you need to set up a structure within which to keep the information. This is known as a *record layout.* If the information contains both words and numbers, the type has to be in "character" or "text" or "alphanumeric" form. If it contains numbers that you might want to add, subtract, divide, or multiply, the type should be "numeric." If the information is a date, use the "date" type, which allows you to calculate the number of days between dates. Choose the data type by clicking on the arrow next to "Text" in "Data Type," and Access will give you a choice of data types.

Unlike a spreadsheet, where you can type without regard to column width, in a database you need to consider how many spaces or characters a field will take (just like a crossword puzzle). Most last names can be contained in 25 characters. State abbreviations always take two characters. Zip codes are

5, 9, or 10 (with a hyphen) characters long. If you choose the numeric type, a database manager generally will make sure you have enough room.

Let's look at how to set up a structure in a database manager. In Access, you click on "New" and then "Design View" in the "Tables" category, as shown in Table 4-25.

**TABLE 4-25**

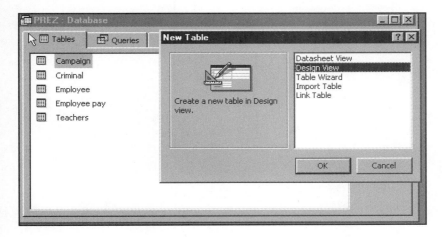

This brings up a grid for you to fill in with the fields, their width, and their type. The grid, or record layout, is shown in Table 4-26. In this sample, you would start creating a table for keeping records of individuals and their birth dates.

**TABLE 4-26**

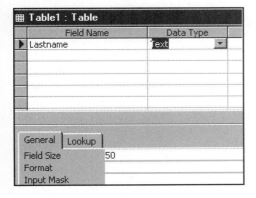

Then you would enter all the fields you want to create and the width and type of these fields. Table 4-27 shows "tablemaking" in progress.

**TABLE 4-27**

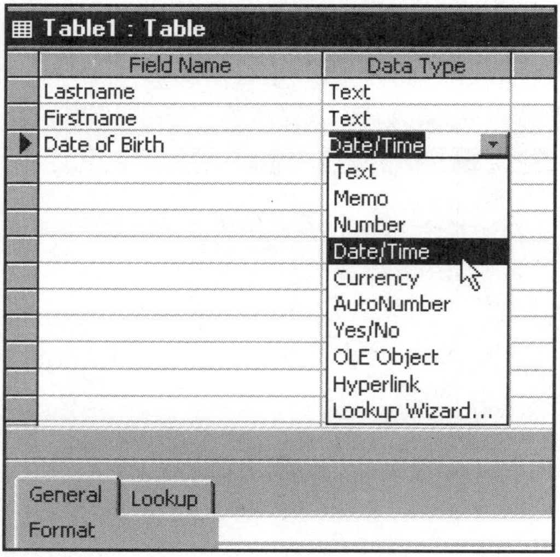

| Field Name | Data Type | |
|---|---|---|
| Lastname | Text | |
| Firstname | Text | |
| Date of Birth | Date/Time ▼ | |

Table1 : Table

Type list:
Text
Memo
Number
Date/Time
Currency
AutoNumber
Yes/No
OLE Object
Hyperlink
Lookup Wizard...

General | Lookup
Format

Once you have the record layout set up, the database manager will let you enter the information.

Over the past decade, many journalists have built their own databases, sometimes matching them to other databases. Two Cincinnati TV reporters built databases to track the resale of badly damaged salvage vehicles and to uncover attendance problems at a county agency. A courts beat reporter in Muskegon, Michigan, created a sentencing database. Dwight Morris of the *Los Angeles Times* oversaw the construction of several massive databases, including one on expenditures made by candidates for Congress. And reporters at the *Seattle Times,* the *Columbus Dispatch,* and the *Hartford Courant* all built databases to track the activity of serial killers.

At the *Hartford Courant* in the early 1990s, two other reporters and I entered into a database demographic information from newspaper clippings about 40 victims—all of whom were female—of unsolved murders. The table we created included the name of each victim, how she was killed, where she was from, and when she was found. Table 4-28 shows some of the fields in our table structure.

**TABLE 4-28**

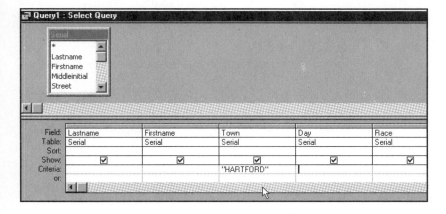

After creating the table, we started to filter the information by selecting the town the victim was from, as shown in Table 4-29.

**TABLE 4-29**

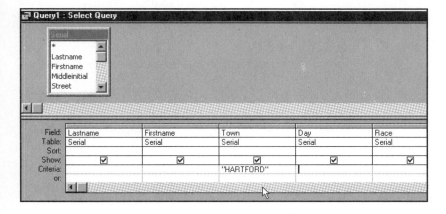

The local police and the medical examiner's office had been investigating the homicides according to the town in which each victim was *found*. But by looking at the town the victim was *from*, we found a pattern that had been overlooked. Table 4-30 shows the first set of names that came up when we searched for victims from Hartford. By examining the detailed information on these women, we found that five of them had last been seen in the same neighborhood. (Note that all the information was not available in every field. Later, we filled it out by using other databases.)

**TABLE 4-30**

| | Lastname | Firstname | Town | Day | Race |
|---|---|---|---|---|---|
| ▶ | MAYO | TAMEIKA | HARTFORD | SUNDAY | B |
| | TERRY | CARLA | HARTFORD | SUNDAY | B |
| | RIVERA | SANDRA | HARTFORD | SUNDAY | H |
| | DANCY | DIEDRE | HARTFORD | | B |
| | PEREZ | EVELYN | HARTFORD | WED | H |
| | UNKNOWN | | HARTFORD | SUNDAY | |
| | PEEBLES | PATRICIA | HARTFORD | TUES | |
| | PARRENO | MARIA | HARTFORD | SAT | H |
| ✳ | | | | | |

We looked at further details of the crimes, interviewed family members, and gathered more information from a medical examiner's database. Law enforcement officials then formed a task force to study possible connections to the killings, which until then had not been linked.

Within a year, some law enforcement officials became convinced that not one but three serial killers were operating in the state. As of the mid-1990s, officials had come close to arresting a suspect. More important, the Hartford killings stopped.

## ■≡ Chapter Summary

- ❏ Database managers handle large numbers of records and allow you to organize the data the way you want.

- ❏ Database managers can quickly create summary data by "grouping" categories of information and allowing you to total the numbers or items in those groups.

- ❏ Database managers can do speedy searches for particular information.

- ❏ Database managers allow you to filter information easily.

- ❏ Database managers allow you to join two or more tables of information by matching names or identification numbers.

- ❏ You can build your own databases using database manager software.

## ■≡ Suggested Tasks

- ❏ Get a database of information about your state or city. *Hint:* If this is difficult, then find a database on the World Wide Web (see Chapter 7) or order one from the National Institute for Computer-Assisted Reporting.

- ❏ Practice selecting certain records by using a criteria.

- ❏ Practice sorting the records.

- ❏ Practice grouping like records together and summing and counting them.

- ❏ Get a relational database from your local officials, or create one of your own.

- ❏ Practice matching the tables in the database, selecting fields from each one, and grouping like records together.

# Mapping:
# Finding Patterns and
# Illustrating the Point

When Hurricane Andrew hit Florida in 1992, the damage was enormous and costly. In the storm's aftermath, the question that occurred to *Miami Herald* computer-assisted reporter Steve Doig was, could any of the destruction have been prevented through better building practices?

Using standard database procedures and mapping software called Atlas GIS, Doig created a map that overlaid wind-speed reports on 60,000 building-inspection damage reports. The visual result was stunning.

One would expect to find that areas that experienced high wind speeds would have significantly greater building damage than would areas with lower wind speeds. But Doig's map showed that some areas with lower wind speeds suffered extensive damage.

Using the map, which later appeared in the paper, Doig and other *Herald* reporters began an investigation into building and inspection practices. They concentrated on construction and inspections done after 1980.

"Mapping is just such a quick and useful way of taking what could be an otherwise unintelligible pile of information and finding the patterns in it," Doig said.

Doig's groundbreaking and inspiring venture is only one example of the hundreds of stories that have benefited from the power of mapping. And, as the software has become less expensive and easier to use, reporters throughout the country have used mapping to reveal patterns of crime, bank and insurance discrimination, landslides, migration, environmental hazards, blighted buildings, health problems, white flight, and bad bridges and dams.

## ■▬▬ TURNING MATCHING SIDEWAYS

The major concept in mapping is the same one we encountered in database managers: matching. In Chapter 4, we represented matching with the visual interface in Microsoft Access. Here, we will substitute categories of information that can be used in mapping. Table 5-1 shows a query from Access that matches the location of dams to a county map by using longitude and latitude.

**TABLE 5-1**

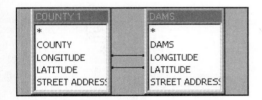

Think of mapping as taking matching in a database and turning it sideways so that you actually put one layer of information on top of another, as in Table 5-2.

**TABLE 5-2**

| Dams | Longitude | Latitude | Street Address |
|------|-----------|----------|----------------|
|      | \|        | \|       |                |
|      | \|        | \|       |                |
|      | \|        | \|       |                |
| County | Longitude | Latitude | Street Address |

Let's illustrate how to do mapping. The software we use in the following examples is ArcView, which is relatively inexpensive. ArcView has become popular because of its friendly interface and because many free maps available on the Internet work in ArcView.

## ▮▬▬ Three Examples

There are countless ways to use mapping in journalism. We will look at the principles behind three of them.

❐ Table 5-3 shows a map of the location of underground petroleum tanks in Columbia, Missouri. Leaking from the tanks has created environmental problems in Missouri. The leak listed as "Wendy's" was beneath a restaurant; when the land was sold to a local church, the leak was discovered and had to be cleaned up.

**TABLE 5-3**

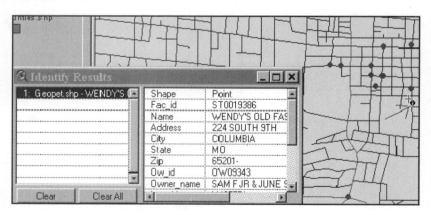

❐ Table 5-4 presents a map of Columbia, showing the location of its dams. Although parts of Columbia tend to flood, the city has no major rivers, and so the number of dams in the area might be surprising to a visitor. You can locate the dams by using the longitude and latitude in the dam database. If you click on the "Identify" button in the menu bar, move the cursor over the dam site, and click, the program gives specific information about one dam. In this case, it's the Woodrail Lake dam.

**TABLE 5-4**

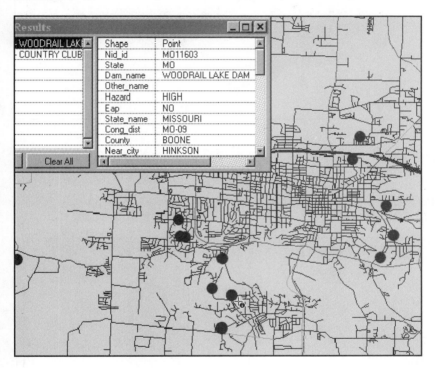

❏ The map in Table 5-5 (p. 78) shows percentage change in population from 1990 to 1996 in every state in the mainland United States. The state with the highest increase has the darkest shading (Nevada), and the states with the greatest decrease have the lightest shading (Connecticut, Rhode Island, North Dakota). This is a good map to use because all the information we need is in a package that comes with ArcView. (All we have to do is a percentage change, which was discussed in Chapter 3.)

**TABLE 5-5**

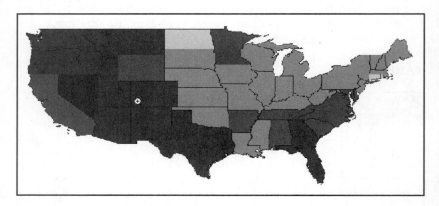

How do we make these maps? First, let's open the ArcView software, click on "File," and click "New Project." You should see the screen shown in Table 5-6.

**TABLE 5-6**                                    **TABLE 5-7**

A *project* is an area created for your work. You can do several maps within a project. We go to "Views," as in Table 5-7, and double-click.

After we double-click and get "View 1," we go up to the tool-bar and click on the plus sign icon under "Edit," which stands for "Add Theme" (see Table 5-8). A *theme* is a map that will act as a template or grid. It's what you will match your data with. In ArcView, the theme could be a map of the states or counties or roads. All these maps are stored in a folder, so you have to know which folder to look in.

**TABLE 5-8**

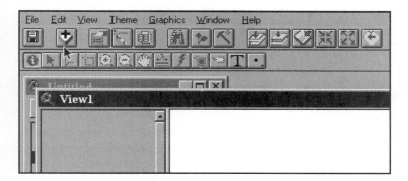

After clicking to add a theme, we go to a folder called "usa," where the counties are known as "counties.shp" (see Table 5-9).

**TABLE 5-9**

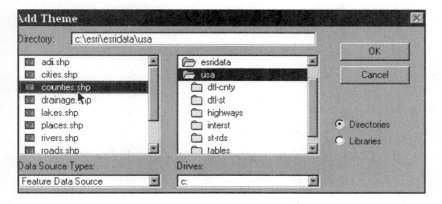

When we add the theme of counties by clicking on "counties.shp," we initially get the way-too-busy map of the United States shown in Table 5-10.

**TABLE 5-10**

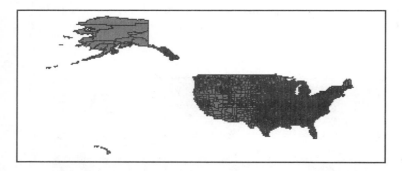

Although our goal is to locate the positions of underground petroleum tanks, what we need to do first is find the Missouri county in which Columbia is located: Boone County. To begin the search, we click on the hammer icon on the toolbar, known as a "Query Builder," as in Table 5-11. (Note that the box by "Counties.shp" in "View" is checked.)

**TABLE 5-11**

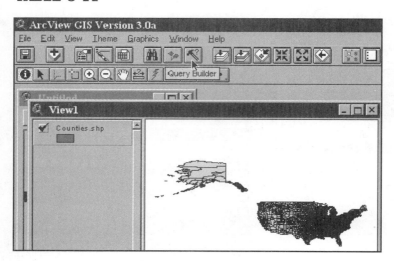

After clicking on the hammer, we get a window, as shown in Table 5-12. We can specify what state we want—Missouri—by highlighting it and then clicking on "New Set."

**TABLE 5-12**

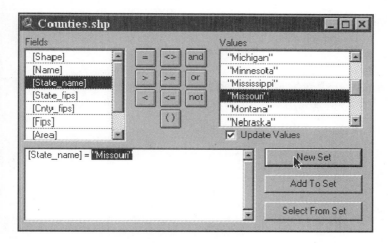

Next, we get the window shown in Table 5-13. We highlight the county—Boone—and then click on "Select From Set."

**TABLE 5-13**

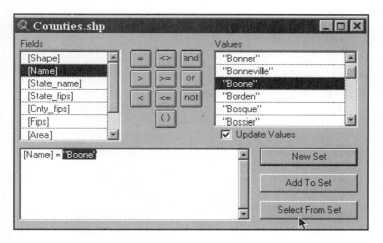

This may seem like a lot of work, but it will be worth it in the end. All we have to do now is go to the "Zoom to Selected" button at the top of Table 5-14 and click on it.

**TABLE 5-14**

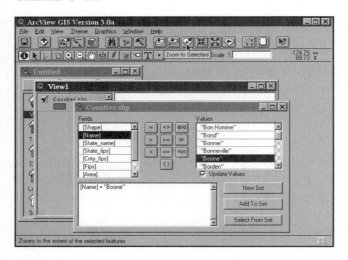

By zooming, as you can see in Table 5-15, we found Boone County. Now, we are ready to put in the maps.

**TABLE 5-15**

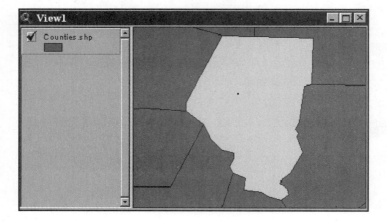

To find the streets we need, we retrieved a digital street map for Boone County. This map was stored in a folder under the title "boone.shp." We clicked on the "Add Theme" icon because whenever we look for a template, we are looking for a theme. We then found "boone.shp" in the folder and double-clicked on it (see Table 5-16).

**TABLE 5-16**

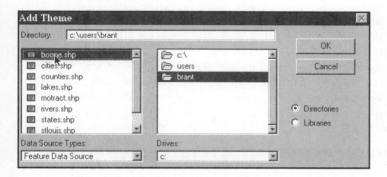

After double-clicking on "boone.shp," we return to our "View" window, and then we click in the box next to "boone.shp," as shown in Table 5-17. This shows us a map of the streets in Boone County, but they're a complex web. We'll soon zoom in on what we need.

**TABLE 5-17**

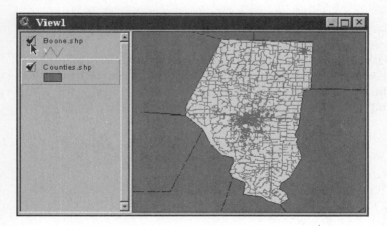

At this point, we have found Boone County and placed the streets in it. Now, we're ready to match our table of storage tanks with the street addresses in Columbia.

Matching a table of information to maps can be easy; it can also be as difficult as any enterprise you might have tried in Chapter 4 on database managers. You don't always get perfect matches; sometimes the addresses are extremely inconsistent and you have to clean them up, and sometimes there are few or no matches.

In the following example, we won't go into excruciating detail. (We'll save that for a Web site exercise.) But we will note the principles.

To get our table, we click on "Tables" in the "View" window, and go to a folder that has the petroleum tank table. We add a table, as shown in Table 5-18.

**TABLE 5-18**

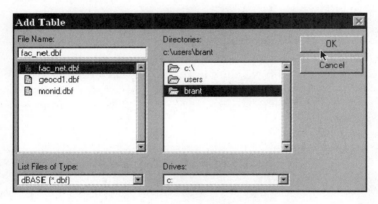

By the way, the state of Missouri's Department of Natural Resources delayed giving us a diskette of this table, but we found it at the department's Web site, downloaded it, and used it for this map. (See Chapter 7 for the download.) The file is called "fac_net.dbf." The "dbf" indicates that the information is already in a database format and can be used in ArcView.

We can view the table before using it. What we see in Table 5-19 is good news: we have the city names and street addresses to match with the Boone County street map.

**TABLE 5-19**

■≡≡ ZOOMING AROUND

Before we continue, let's do a little more zooming with the magnifying glass found in the toolbar. We click on the magnifying glass and put the cursor on the map (shown in Table 5-17, p. 83). Next, we drag the magnifier around to get a close-up of part of the area and then drag the magnifying glass around the selected area. We do this several times, and in Table 5-20 (p. 86), you can see that we are getting closer to downtown Columbia.

**TABLE 5-20**

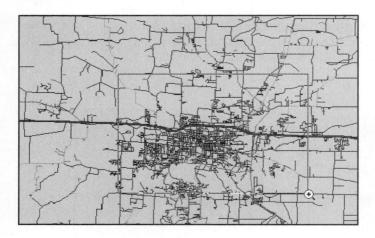

Next, we want to match the addresses. As shown in Table 5-21, we go to "View" in the menu and click on "Geocode Addresses."

**TABLE 5-21**

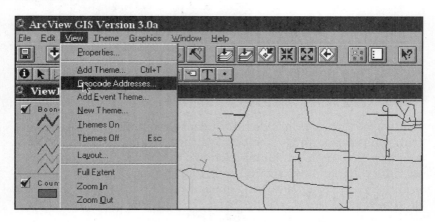

This takes us to one of our matches. As you can see, our reference theme in Table 5-22 is "Boone.shp" (the street addresses). The "Address Table"—the one we want to match

**TABLE 5-22**

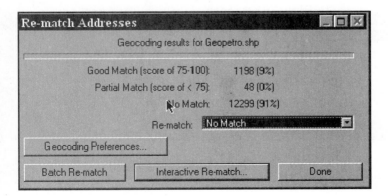

with—is "fac_net.dbf." In this match, we use the address field
(*field* is the same as *column* or *category*), and for "Zone Field" we
use "Zip." When we are ready, we click on "Batch Match."

Now, when we ran our match this way, the street addresses
were matched, but the city was not properly matched. (Street-
address matching always requires some adjusting.) We then run
the geocode addresses again on petroleum tanks, limiting the
run to the city of Columbia.

When we run the "Batch Match" this time, we get the result
screen shown in Table 5-23.

**TABLE 5-23**

The number of matches is still on the high side. However, after further adjustment, we get a pretty accurate result, with dots representing where the tanks are. If we want to, we can label the streets, or we can use the "Identify" button in the top left of Table 5-24 to get information on one of the tanks.

**TABLE 5-24**

If we click on the "i" and move the cursor to the proper tank and click, we see the information for the Wendy's site, as shown in Table 5-25.

**TABLE 5-25**

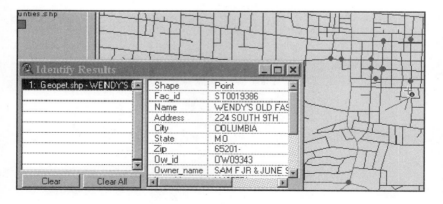

## ▣▤ LONGITUDE AND LATITUDE FOR THE DAM DATA

Without repeating all the steps we took in the petroleum-tanks example, let's map the location of dams in the Columbia area by using longitude and latitude. After adding the dams table, known as "monid.dbf," we go to the "View" button in the menu bar and hit "Add Event." When we get this window, we fill in the "X field" with longitude and the "Y field" with latitude, as in Table 5-26.

**TABLE 5-26**

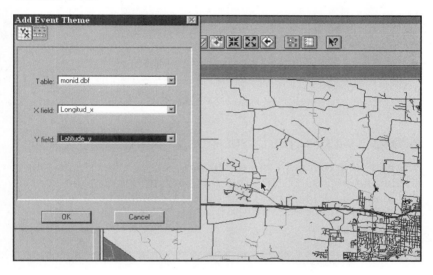

By matching the longitude and latitude in the dams table to the longitude and latitude in the county map, we locate the dams in Boone County (see Table 5-27, p. 90). We can now pick out information for one dam if we want to.

**TABLE 5-27**

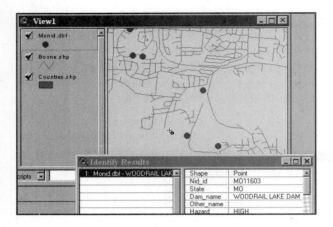

## TRACKING THE POPULATION IN STATES

We can add the map of the United States now by adding a theme, as in Table 5-28. This information is generally kept in the "esridata" folder that comes with ArcView.

**TABLE 5-28**

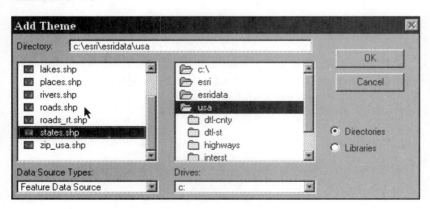

Once we have chosen the theme of states, we click on "Tables" in the "View" window. The statistics that come up with that map are shown in Table 5-29.

**TABLE 5-29**

| State_fips | Sub_region | State_abb | Pop1990 | Pop1996 |
|---|---|---|---|---|
| 53 | Pacific | WA | 4866692 | 5629613 |
| 30 | Mtn | MT | 799065 | 885762 |
| 23 | N Eng | ME | 1227928 | 1254465 |
| 38 | W N Cen | ND | 638800 | 633534 |
| 46 | W N Cen | SD | 696004 | 721374 |
| 56 | Mtn | WY | 453588 | 487142 |
| 55 | E N Cen | WI | 4891769 | 5144123 |
| 16 | Mtn | ID | 1006749 | 1201327 |
| 50 | N Eng | VT | 562758 | 587726 |
| 27 | W N Cen | MN | 4375099 | 4639933 |
| 41 | Pacific | OR | 2842321 | 3203820 |
| 33 | N Eng | NH | 1109252 | 1156932 |

Once we have determined that we have population statistics, ArcView will allow us to create a new field and to calculate the percentage change in population in each state. After that, we can go to the "Legend Editor," which will automatically divide the percentages into five groups and color code them for us. This is shown in Table 5-30 on p. 92 (this window is so large we had to put it on the next page).

The result is the map in Table 5-31, which shows where the population is changing in the United States. (Gradations of shading, from lightest to darkest, indicate, respectively, the greatest decrease to the greatest increase in population.)

**TABLE 5-31**

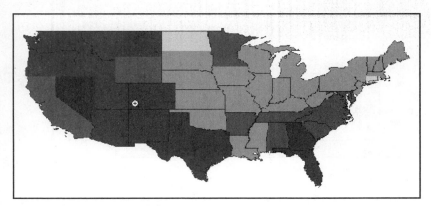

**TABLE 5-30**

| | | | | |
|---|---|---|---|---|
| **Legend Editor** | | | _ □ X | |
| Theme: | States.shp | ▼ | Load... | |
| Legend Type: | Graduated Color | ▼ | Save... | |
| | | | Default | |
| Classification Field: | percent change | ▼ | Classify... | |
| Normalize by: | <None> | ▼ | | |

| Symbol | Value | Label |
|---|---|---|
| | -0.09 - 0 | -0.09 - 0 |
| | 0 - 0.05 | 0 - 0.05 |
| | 0.05 - 0.1 | 0.05 - 0.1 |
| | 0.1 - 0.19 | 0.1 - 0.19 |
| | 0.19 - 0.27 | 0.19 - 0.27 |

Color Ramps: Red monochromatic

Advanced... | Statistics... | Undo | Apply

| Pop1990 | Pop1996 | change | percent change |
|---|---|---|---|
| 4866692 | 5629613 | 762921 | 0.16 |
| 799065 | 885762 | 86697 | 0.11 |
| 1227928 | 1254465 | 26537 | 0.02 |
| 638800 | 633534 | -5266 | -0.01 |
| 696004 | 721374 | 25370 | 0.04 |
| 453588 | 487142 | 33554 | 0.07 |
| 4891769 | 5144123 | 252354 | 0.05 |
| 1006749 | 1201327 | 194578 | 0.19 |
| 562758 | 587726 | 24968 | 0.04 |
| 4375099 | 4639933 | 264834 | 0.06 |
| 2842321 | 3203820 | 361499 | 0.13 |
| 1109252 | 1156932 | 47680 | 0.04 |

It's not too difficult to imagine all the applications of mapping software, especially for local stories. Ron Campbell of the *Orange County Register* in California used it to show how banks had retreated from the most impoverished area of the county. Using a database of bank branch addresses and mapping those addresses, Campbell showed there were 200,000 people who did not have easy access to a bank. By overlaying census data, he also showed that they live in a low to moderate income area.

Reporters at other newspapers and TV stations use the street addresses of incidents of crime to show where and what kind of crime is occurring in their communities.

Penny Loeb at *U.S. News and World Report* used layers of mortgage data, bank branches, and insurance data to show how banks and insurers had retreated from racially diverse and impoverished areas of cities.

Often, a computer-assisted story can be too filled with numbers. Mapping can make the point of the story quickly apparent by translating those numbers into pictures.

## ◼≡≡≡ CHAPTER SUMMARY

❐ Mapping software is used to decipher complicated information.

❐ Mapping uses the principles and skills employed in database managers and spreadsheets.

❐ Many free maps are available on the Internet.

❐ Mapping software can use street addresses, longitude and latitude, and geographic areas.

❐ Maps are a good way to summarize numbers and visually make the point of the story.

## ◼≡≡≡ SUGGESTED TASKS

❐ Look for maps in a newspaper or TV report. How do they help the story?

❐ List five local stories that could use maps.

❐ Find or buy mapping software, and do the exercise (presented in this chapter) on population change in the United States.

# A Few Words about Statistics:
# A Brief Foray into
# Social Research Tools

> Today journalists might do well to dream the following
> dreams: they might dream of taking over from social sci-
> entists, during what everyone agrees is a dismal, petty,
> doctrinaire time in the academy, as the leading explain-
> ers of American society; and they might dream of accom-
> plishing all three goals—of being portraitist, investigator,
> and explainer—at the same time, in the same work.[1]

Nicholas Lemann, author of *The Promised Land: The Great Black Migration and How It Changed America*, wrote this in the *IRE Journal* in 1991. It now looks as if more and more journalists are starting to move toward that dream, using some of the methods and statistical analysis techniques of social scientists.

But if spreadsheets make journalists uncomfortable, the subject of statistics has often generated outright terror. Many journalists report on statistics every day, but have a less-than-complete understanding of them. Others avoid statistics, even though using a few basic analytic tools could give them good clues and directions about a story.

Yet, as journalists become more computer savvy, they become more number savvy. As they become more number savvy, they

---

[1] Lemann, N. Ordinary People and Extraordinary Journalism. *The IRE Journal* (December 1991), p. 7.

become more statistics savvy. Journalists constantly compare and measure, and statistics—as social science researchers have long shown—provide good tools for doing just that.

Furthermore, acquiring basic statistical skills is important for journalists who want to flourish in the 21st century. "Statistics are used or misused even by people who tell us, 'I don't believe in statistics,' then claim that all of us or most people or many do such and such," wrote journalist Victor Cohn in his excellent book, *News & Numbers*. "The question for reporters is, how should we not merely repeat such numbers, stated or implied, but also interpret them to deliver the best possible picture of reality?"[2]

Philip Meyer, a veteran reporter and pioneer in the computer-assisted field, said in his 1991 book, *The New Precision Journalism*, "They are raising the ante on what it takes to be a journalist."[3] Meyer, who teaches at the University of North Carolina, has used social science research methods for years in his consulting work for news organizations. The rest of the journalism community is finally catching up with him.

This chapter will examine only a few of the basic descriptive statistics and methods. Consider it a prelude to reading in-depth books such as Meyer's and Cohn's and taking courses in statistics.

A journalist needs to go cautiously when dealing with statistics for the first time. Social science researchers have become concerned about journalists misinterpreting and misusing statistical methods—not through malice but through ignorance. Any journalist using statistical methods should expect a debate over his or her numbers and interpretations after a story appears.

But that shouldn't prevent journalists from learning certain measurements as a way of reviewing data and as a device to keep them from making erroneous assumptions. For example, Alan Cox, who does computer-assisted reporting at WCCO-TV in Minneapolis, runs statistical checks on databases to avoid making incorrect assumptions. Other reporters use statistical

---

[2] Cohn, Victor. *News & Numbers*. Ames, IA. Iowa State University Press, 1989, p. 4.

[3] Meyer, Philip. *The New Precision Journalism*. Bloomington, IN. Indiana University Press, 1991, p. 1.

methods to better judge the performance of schools, to examine the quality of medical treatment at hospitals, or to judge the fairness of property taxes.

## ▥ Three Ways of Looking at Data

You may remember that Chapter 3 opened with a discussion of the fire department story by Christopher Schmitt of the *San Jose Mercury News*. The story not only demonstrated the effective use of a spreadsheet, but it also highlighted the fallacy of looking at just "the average." To deal with numbers, journalists should know the three most common ways of summarizing a collection of numbers: mean, median, and mode.

❑ *Mean* is what is commonly called the average.

❑ *Median* is the middle value, or the point which half the numbers fall above and half the numbers fall below. (If there is a tie, it gets a little tricky, but a spreadsheet can do the calculation for you.)

❑ *Mode* is the most frequent value in the database—that is, the value that occurs most frequently when you look at the data.

Neill Borowski, head of computer-assisted reporting at the *Philadelphia Inquirer,* used a good example of statistical misunderstanding at a national conference. He said that baseball fans were outraged by players' salaries because they had heard the average salary was $1.2 million. But the median salary, the amount that half the salaries exceed and half fall below, was $500,000, and the mode, or the most frequent salary, was $109,000. The numbers indicate that only a few players are making really big money. If you asked all baseball players to raise their hands when their salary was announced, the largest number (the mode, not the majority) of hands would go up for $109,000. (Okay, it's still a lot, but it's being earned by people who generally have 10 years or less to make most of their money.)

Journalists want to represent numbers as fairly as possible, and the mean, median, and mode give them a chance to do so. If a journalist obtains a set of salaries or house prices or test scores, he or she needs to consider what the fairest representation is. If the numbers are relatively close together, the mean (or average) is a reasonable way to summarize them. But if the numbers are spread out, a journalist should be sure not to skew the summary.

For example, Table 6-1 shows 10 salaries.

| TABLE 6-1 | |
|---|---|
| Jill | 1,000,000 |
| Ben | 30,000 |
| John | 40,000 |
| Ellen | 25,000 |
| Doris | 30,000 |
| Dick | 45,000 |
| Milly | 30,000 |
| Rhonda | 40,000 |
| Max | 40,000 |
| Gigi | 40,000 |

If you put these salaries into a spreadsheet, you can find the mean, median, and mode. As shown in Table 6-2, you can do all three as you did when summing a column in Chapter 3. You type: "=AVERAGE(B3:B12)" in B14; "=MEDIAN(B3:B12)" in B15; and "=MODE(B3:B12)" in B16. The results are shown in Table 6-2.

**TABLE 6-2**

| | A | B |
|---|---|---|
| 1 | Name | Salary |
| 2 | | |
| 3 | Jill | $ 1,000,000 |
| 4 | Ben | $ 30,000 |
| 5 | John | $ 40,000 |
| 6 | Ellen | $ 25,000 |
| 7 | Doris | $ 30,000 |
| 8 | Dick | $ 45,000 |
| 9 | Milly | $ 30,000 |
| 10 | Rhonda | $ 40,000 |
| 11 | Max | $ 40,000 |
| 12 | Gigi | $ 40,000 |
| 13 | | |
| 14 | Mean | $ 132,000 |
| 15 | Median | $ 40,000 |
| 16 | Mode | $ 40,000 |

The mean, or average, salary is $132,000. But nine individuals don't come within $85,000 of this. The median is $40,000, and the mode is $40,000. Which measurement is more representative and fair?

In this example, Jill's salary would be considered an "outlier." In social research parlance, an *outlier* is a number that is either extremely small or large in relation to other numbers in a database.

Jill, the chief executive of the corporation, makes 25 times the median wage. You might want to know why, and whether there is a possible story here.

When you examine a few databases closely, you begin to regard outliers with healthy suspicion. Outliers are often too good to be true. They frequently turn out to be the result of data-entry errors (which will be examined in Chapter 9). The usual explanation is that someone put in an extra zero by mistake, for example, and Jill's salary is actually $100,000.

Social researchers suggest that you look carefully at the outliers and consider discarding them, especially if you expect to work with averages. This doesn't mean you can't bring the outliers back later. You might be looking at state data and notice that one county has highly unusual numbers. So you examine all the counties but that one in your first analysis, and then look at all the counties together to see why that one county distorts the numbers.

For example, when Jack Ewing, a court reporter at the *Hartford Courant,* and I looked at racial disparities in bail for criminal defendants in Connecticut in the early 1990s, we examined the average bail for blacks and Hispanics versus that for whites. However, on the advice of some wise social researchers, we limited the bail to amounts above zero and equal to or below $100,000. (We got rid of zero because it meant no bail was set. We held to $100,000 and below because there were a few amounts well above $100,000 that could have distorted the results.) We found that black and Hispanic males, on average, received much higher bail—70 percent or more—than did whites for the same kind of felony.

Then we went back and looked at the outliers. It turned out that an unusual number of high bail amounts were being given to blacks in one courthouse. In fact, blacks were getting higher bail amounts for drug charges—as much as $1 million—than some whites were getting for murder.

Later, a judge in New Haven acknowledged that he was giving out high bail to persons accused of drug offenses because he didn't think they spent enough time in jail once they were convicted. Thus, his solution was to lock up the presumed innocent. Unfortunately, the judge was contributing to his own frustration because, when he kept people in jail awaiting trial, it created prison overcrowding—which led to the early release of those serving time.

## ■▬▬ Standard Deviation

Another handy statistical tool is the standard deviation. The *standard deviation* tells how much the numbers vary around the average. For example, in the bail story, the standard deviation for bail amounts set by judges indicated that the amount for blacks varied widely. This led to questions about whether the judges were following their own guidelines.

Fortunately, we don't have to calculate standard deviation; statistical software does it for us.

Statistics should serve as safeguards. Rather than make journalists leap to conclusions, statistics should prompt journalists to question the veracity of their perceptions and assumptions or those of the people the journalists are covering.

## ■▬▬ Frequencies

One good statistical software tool is *frequencies*. Frequencies are more efficient than spreadsheets or database managers, and they allow you to do in one step what can take two steps otherwise: counting kinds of records, and then calculating the percentage of each of those counts.

For example, many journalists cut their statistical teeth on an annual home mortgage loan database from the Federal Reserve. The database, created by the Home Mortgage Disclosure

Act, contains information on loan applications, including ethnicity, income, and action taken by the lender.

Table 6-3 shows a slice of 10,802 records on loan applicants from part of Tennessee. (The records have been simplified and the ethnicity changed from numerical codes to "black" and "white" for this discussion.)

**TABLE 6-3**

| 1:ethnic | 🔳 | | | |
|---|---|---|---|---|
| | **ethnic** | **income** | **loanamt** | **action** | **name** |
| **1** | white | 27 | 48 | Denied | SECURITY BANK, SSB |
| **2** | black | 41 | 72 | Denied | SECURITY BANK, SSB |
| **3** | white | 42 | 75 | Loaned | SECURITY BANK, SSB |
| **4** | black | 30 | 65 | Denied | SECURITY BANK, SSB |
| **5** | white | 32 | 74 | Loaned | SECURITY BANK, SSB |
| **6** | white | 25 | 59 | Loaned | SECURITY BANK, SSB |

"Ethnic" is the ethnicity of the applicant, and "action" is the action taken by the financial institution. The monetary amounts are given in thousands, so that "27" is actually $27,000. In Table 6-3, the data is presented using the statistical software SPSS (Statistical Software for the Political and Social Sciences). SPSS and SAS (Statistical Analysis System) are the two pieces of statistical software used most frequently by journalists. SPSS is more popular because it is less expensive, but both are strong programs. Note that although you are looking at statistical software, you are still in the two-dimensional world. Columns and rows still exist, but the language is different. In statistical software, the columns are called "variables" instead of "fields," and the rows are called "observations."

Why use statistical software? Well, once you are comfortable with spreadsheets and database managers, you will find that statistical software does some of the calculations and filtering more quickly. It also allows you to explore a database more thoroughly.

For example, you might want to get an idea of how many loan applicants are black, Hispanic, or white. This concept is the same as "group by" in the chapter on databases, but with statistical software you can get not only a count of each ethnicity but also a percentage.

First, go to the menu bar at the top of the screen, click on "Statistics," as shown in Table 6-4. Then click on "Summarize."

**TABLE 6-4**

| TnHMDA - SPSS Data Editor |
|---|

File  Edit  View  Data  Transform  **Statistics**  Graphs  Utilities  Window

Summarize ▶
Custom Tables ▶
Compare Means ▶
General Linear Model ▶
Correlate ▶
Regression ▶
Loglinear ▶
Classify ▶
Data Reduction ▶
Scale ▶
Nonparametric Tests ▶
Time Series ▶
Survival ▶

1:ethnic

| | ethnic | income | tion |
|---|---|---|---|
| 1 | white | | ied |
| 2 | black | | ied |
| 3 | white | | ned |
| 4 | black | | ied |
| 5 | white | | ned |

When you click on "Summarize," you get a menu headed by "Frequencies," as shown in Table 6-5.

**TABLE 6-5**

| TnHMDA - SPSS Data Editor |
|---|

File  Edit  View  Data  Transform  Statistics  Graphs  Utilities  Window  Help

Summarize ▶ → Frequencies...
Custom Tables ▶  Descriptives...
Compare Means ▶  Explore...
General Linear Model ▶  Crosstabs...
Correlate ▶
Regression ▶  Case Summaries...
Loglinear ▶  Report Summaries in Rows...
Classify ▶  Report Summaries in Columns...
Data Reduction ▶
Scale ▶
Nonparametric Tests ▶
Time Series ▶
Survival ▶
Multiple Response ▶
Missing Value Analysis...

1:ethnic

| | ethnic | income | | | |
|---|---|---|---|---|---|
| 1 | white | | | | |
| 2 | black | | | | SECURITY BANK, SSB |
| 3 | white | | | ned | SECURITY BANK, SSB |
| 4 | black | | | ied | SECURITY BANK, SSB |
| 5 | white | | | ned | SECURITY BANK, SSB |
| 6 | white | | | ned | SECURITY BANK, SSB |
| 7 | white | 17 | 52 | Denied | SECURITY BANK, SSB |

When you click on "Frequencies," you see a screen like the one in Table 6-6.

**TABLE 6-6**

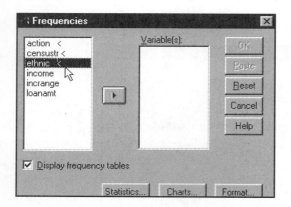

This screen allows you to choose the column (or variable) that you want to count. In this case, the variable is "ethnic." To move "ethnic" from the box on the left to the "Variable(s)" box, click on "ethnic," and then click on the arrow between the boxes. The result is shown in Table 6-7.

**TABLE 6-7**

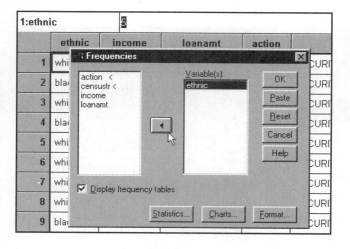

Once you have selected "ethnic," hit the "OK" button. In Table 6-8, you see the result. SPSS has counted each ethnicity. The "Frequency" column gives the actual count of each record for an applicant, and the next two columns give the percentage of the total. (By the way, SPSS also indicates that an ethnicity is filled in for each applicant because there are no "Missing" cases.)

**TABLE 6-8**

**➡ Frequencies**

**Statistics**

|  | N | |
|---|---|---|
|  | Valid | Missing |
| ethnic | 10802 | 0 |

**ethnic**

|  |  | Frequency | Percent | Valid Percent | Cumulative Percent |
|---|---|---|---|---|---|
| Valid | black | 874 | 8.1 | 8.1 | 8.1 |
|  | white | 9928 | 91.9 | 91.9 | 100.0 |
|  | Total | 10802 | 100.0 | 100.0 |  |
| Total |  | 10802 | 100.0 |  |  |

You can see from Table 6-8 that most of the applicants are white. Although the number of black applicants is relatively small, there are enough black applicants for you to continue your work.

## DESCRIPTIVE STATISTICS

The next step in exploring the database is to determine the averages of loan amount and income. Once again, go to "Statistics" and then "Summarize," but this time choose "Descriptives," as shown in Table 6-9.

**TABLE 6-9**

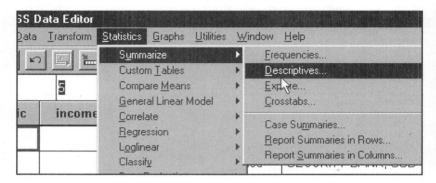

This will allow you to find the averages of applicants' loan amounts and incomes. At the same time, you might want to know what the lowest and highest amounts are and what the standard deviation (or "spread" around the average) looks like. Table 6-10 shows the two columns—"income" and "loanamt"—that are numeric and for which you can do calculations.

**TABLE 6-10**

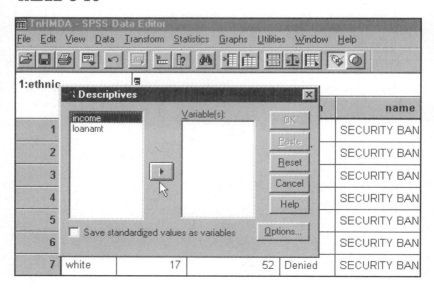

Move "income" and "loanamt" to the "Variable(s)" box by clicking on each one and then clicking on the arrow between the two boxes (see Table 6-11).

**TABLE 6-11**

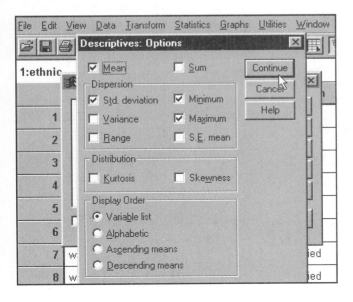

Then, click on the "Options" button at the bottom of the screen to decide what kinds of calculations you want. The software gives you several choices. You should choose "Mean," "Minimum," "Maximum," and "Std. deviation" (see Table 6-12), because these measurements will give you a quick look at the numbers.

**TABLE 6-12**

Then hit "Continue" and then "OK," and return to the original screen, and hit "OK" again. The results are shown in Table 6-13.

**TABLE 6-13**

➡ **Descriptives**

**Descriptive Statistics**

|  | N | Minimum | Maximum | Mean | Std. Deviation |
|---|---|---|---|---|---|
| INCOME | 10802 | 10 | 996 | 59.12 | 62.82 |
| LOANAMT | 10802 | 1 | 990 | 91.33 | 75.76 |
| Valid N (listwise) | 10802 |  |  |  |  |

You can see that the average income is $59,120, the minimum income is $10,000, and the maximum income is $996,000. For amount of loans, the average is $91,330, the minimum is $1,000, and the maximum is $990,000. The standard deviations are $62,820 for income and $75,760 for loan amount.

This look at the database also indicates that there are some potential outliers. The $1,000 figure could be due to data-entry errors or special cases, which means that you will have to contact the source of the database. The high numbers for loans and incomes are probably numbers that you want to throw out when making comparisons; there are so few of them, and they could distort your results.

There is a handy tool called a "histogram" that lets you see how data are distributed. It's found under "Graphs" in the SPSS menu and is not difficult to use. Table 6-14 gives a histogram for income. Note that there are far fewer salaries on the right, where the amounts are high.

**TABLE 6-14**

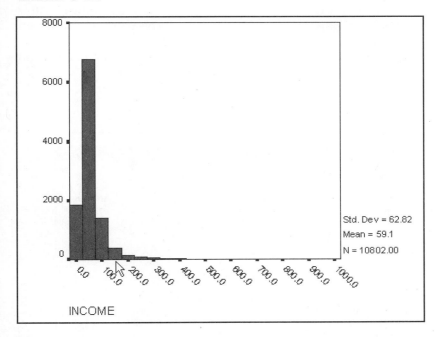

You can examine the data in more depth by using another part of the program, called "Explore." Note how SPSS leads you through this step by step. Logically, you do "Frequencies" first, then "Descriptives," and then "Explore" (see Table 6-15).

**TABLE 6-15**

At this point, you have the ability to come up with many more statistics than you need or initially can understand. After clicking on "Explore," you put "ethnic," the category by which you want to group the data, in the "Factor List." You place the fields you want to perform calculations on—"loanamt" and "income"—in the "Dependent List." (See Table 6-16.)

**TABLE 6-16**

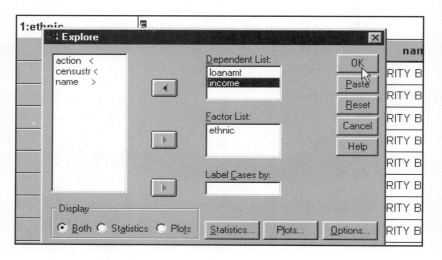

Don't worry about the language. This procedure is the same as grouping in a database manager.

When you hit "OK" here, you see an initially confusing list of numbers for each ethnicity. But if you look closely, you can see the numbers in which you are interested. Table 6-17 shows loan amounts for blacks.

**TABLE 6-17**

| Descriptives | | | | Statistic | Std. Error |
|---|---|---|---|---|---|
| ethnic | | | | | |
| LOANAMT | black | Mean | | 80.17 | 2.15 |
| | | 95% Confidence Interval for Mean | Lower Bound | 75.95 | |
| | | | Upper Bound | 84.39 | |
| | | 5% Trimmed Mean | | 73.33 | |
| | | Median | | 67.00 | |
| | | Variance | | 4043.072 | |
| | | Std. Deviation | | 63.59 | |
| | | Minimum | | 4 | |
| | | Maximum | | 960 | |
| | | Range | | 956 | |
| | | Interquartile Range | | 53.00 | |
| | | Skewness | | 4.669 | .083 |
| | | Kurtosis | | 46.772 | .165 |

Table 6-18 shows loan amounts for whites.

**TABLE 6-18**

| | white | | | 92.31 | .77 |
|---|---|---|---|---|---|
| | | Mean | | 92.31 | .77 |
| | | 95% Confidence Interval for Mean | Lower Bound | 90.80 | |
| | | | Upper Bound | 93.82 | |
| | | 5% Trimmed Mean | | 83.37 | |
| | | Median | | 74.00 | |
| | | Variance | | 5877.182 | |
| | | Std. Deviation | | 76.66 | |
| | | Minimum | | 1 | |
| | | Maximum | | 990 | |
| | | Range | | 989 | |
| | | Interquartile Range | | 72.00 | |
| | | Skewness | | 2.959 | .025 |
| | | Kurtosis | | 15.681 | .049 |

Let's look at a couple of comparisons. The mean loan amount for blacks is approximately $80,170. The mean loan amount for whites is approximately $92,310. The median amount for blacks is $67,000, and the median for whites is $74,000. Now take a look at incomes for blacks, as shown in Table 6-19.

**TABLE 6-19**

| INCOME | black | Mean | | 46.03 | 1.53 |
|---|---|---|---|---|---|
| | | 95% Confidence Interval for Mean | Lower Bound | 43.03 | |
| | | | Upper Bound | 49.03 | |
| | | 5% Trimmed Mean | | 40.50 | |
| | | Median | | 36.00 | |
| | | Variance | | 2041.944 | |
| | | Std. Deviation | | 45.19 | |
| | | Minimum | | 10 | |
| | | Maximum | | 740 | |
| | | Range | | 730 | |
| | | Interquartile Range | | 29.00 | |
| | | Skewness | | 7.294 | .083 |
| | | Kurtosis | | 84.375 | .165 |

Table 6-20 shows incomes for whites.

**TABLE 6-20**

| white | Mean | | 60.28 | .64 |
|---|---|---|---|---|
| | 95% Confidence Interval for Mean | Lower Bound | 59.02 | |
| | | Upper Bound | 61.54 | |
| | 5% Trimmed Mean | | 51.24 | |
| | Median | | 44.00 | |
| | Variance | | 4098.001 | |
| | Std. Deviation | | 64.02 | |
| | Minimum | | 10 | |
| | Maximum | | 996 | |
| | Range | | 986 | |
| | Interquartile Range | | 39.00 | |
| | Skewness | | 5.678 | .025 |
| | Kurtosis | | 52.219 | .049 |

The mean income for blacks is approximately $46,030, and the median income is $36,000. The mean income for whites is $60,280, and the median income is $44,000. Let's do two quick calculations comparing both means and medians.

Comparing the mean income for blacks to the loan amounts for blacks shows that black mean income is 57 percent of the loan amount. Doing the same for whites shows that white mean income is 65 percent of the loan amount.

Comparing black median income to black loan amount shows that black median income is 54 percent of the loan amount sought, whereas for whites the median income is 59 percent of the loan amount. In other words, both whites and blacks are applying for loans about 1.5 to 1.9 times higher than their annual incomes.

In either comparison, there isn't much difference between blacks and whites when considering what an applicant's income is and the amount of loan the applicant is seeking. So it doesn't appear that either group is asking for loan amounts that far exceed their incomes.

## ▣▤▤ CROSSTABS

Now you want to determine how denial rates compare. In other words, what percentage of blacks are denied loans as compared to whites?

One quick way to start in statistical software is by using crosstabs. Crosstabs, which are like an extension of frequencies, permit a journalist to get an overall view of data in several ways. A *crosstab* allows you to compare different categories of information (or "variables"). When you set up crosstabs of two variables, think about the "cause" variable and "effect" variable. (Social researchers call them the "independent" variable and the "dependent" variable.)

Generally, the independent variable goes in the column and the dependent variable goes in the row. In analyzing whether a person might be denied a home loan on the basis of ethnicity, *ethnicity* is the independent variable, and the *action* of the home loan application is the dependent variable.

Does one's success in obtaining a loan depend on one's ethnic background? It's easier to show this than to explain it. In the following example, the focus is on home loans in the Nashville, Tennessee, area in 1995. (The database has been altered to make it easier to understand. The database comes with ethnicity and the action of financial institutions in numeric codes. SPSS allows you to convert those codes into words fairly easily. Also, only blacks and whites will be compared.)

Table 6-21 shows how to proceed. Go back to "Statistics," then choose "Summarize," and then choose "Crosstabs."

**TABLE 6-21**

Click on "Crosstabs." You will get a familiar screen that gives a choice of variables to use (see Table 6-22). Put "ethnic," the independent variable, in the "Column(s)" box. Then put "action" (the action by the lender) in the "Row(s)" box.

**TABLE 6-22**

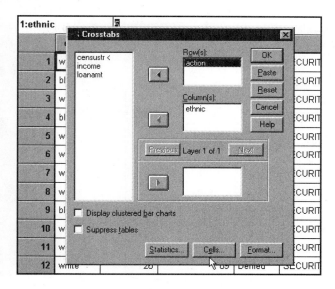

At the bottom of the screen, there are several choices. Click on "Cells," and you will see more choices, as shown in Table 6-23.

**TABLE 6-23**

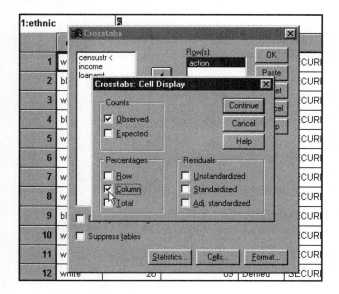

Clicking on "Column" will give the percentages of denials of loans for each ethnic group. Return to the main screen by hitting "Continue," and then hit "OK." You will see a display as shown in Table 6-24.

**TABLE 6-24**

| Loan action * ethnic Crosstabulation | | | | | |
|---|---|---|---|---|---|
| | | | ethnic | | Total |
| | | | black | white | |
| Loan action | Loaned | Count | 399 | 6205 | 6604 |
| | | % within ethnic | 45.7% | 62.5% | 61.1% |
| | Approved | Count | 67 | 990 | 1057 |
| | | % within ethnic | 7.7% | 10.0% | 9.8% |
| | Denied | Count | 408 | 2733 | 3141 |
| | | % within ethnic | 46.7% | 27.5% | 29.1% |
| Total | | Count | 874 | 9928 | 10802 |
| | | % within ethnic | 100.0% | 100.0% | 100.0% |

As you can see, 46.7 percent of black applicants were denied loans, as were 27.5 percent of whites. Now, recall the income differences from one of your descriptive statistics. Is there a way to flatten out some of those differences? Yes.

Statistical software allows you to routinely create ranges of such items as income. Here's how. Click on "Transform," then on "Recode," and then on "Into Different Variables." The result is shown in Table 6-25.

**TABLE 6-25**

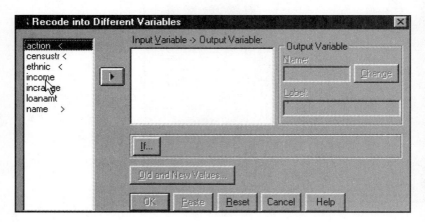

This may seem a little complicated at first, so go slowly. As shown in Table 6-26, click on "income" as the numeric variable containing the information you want to consolidate into ranges. Then, type "incrange" (income range) under "Output Variable." This is the name of a new column you will create. Then, click on the "If" button.

**TABLE 6-26**

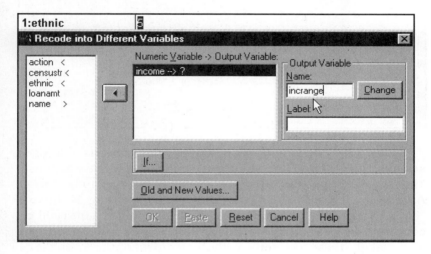

Table 6-27 (p. 116) shows the result. Now type:

incomes > 0 and income <= 150

This means that you will keep in your new database all incomes that are greater than 0 and less than or equal to $150,000. This will rid your calculations of the most extreme "outliers."

**TABLE 6-27**

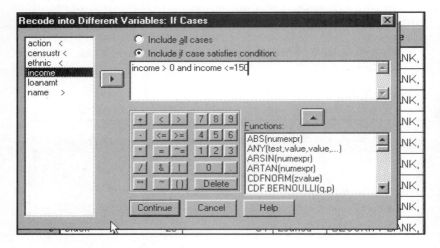

Click on "Continue" to return to the previous "Recode" screen (Table 6-26), and then click on "Old and New Values." This is where you start converting various incomes into ranges. As shown in Table 6-28, you can start by typing in (under "Range") that every income between $1,000 and $25,000 will be converted (as shown under "New Value") to $25,000. (You can also "label" these columns with better descriptions, such as "1to25"—but that's another series of keystrokes.)

**TABLE 6-28**

Hit "Add," and then type in the next range ("26 through 50"), as shown in Table 6-29.

**TABLE 6-29**

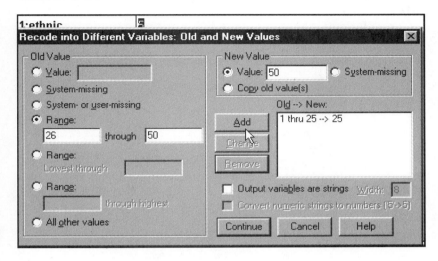

Here, you are converting all incomes from $26,000 through $50,000, to $50,000. As you continue, Table 6-30 shows the progression of the conversion.

**TABLE 6-30**

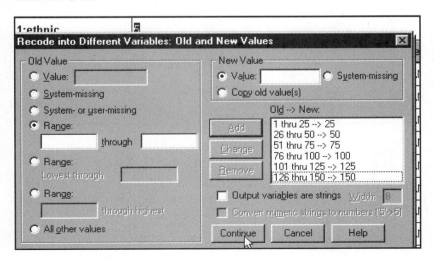

Once the conversions are complete, you click "Continue" and return to the previous screen (shown in Table 6-31). Now click "OK."

**TABLE 6-31**

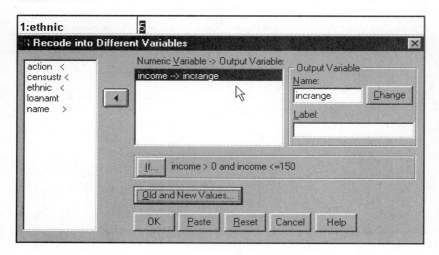

| 1:ethnic | 5 |

The revised database with its new column ("incrange") is shown in Table 6-32.

**TABLE 6-32**

| 1:incrange | 50 | | | | | | |
|---|---|---|---|---|---|---|---|
| | ethnic | income | loanamt | action | name | censustr | incrange |
| 1 | white | 27 | 48 | Denied | SECURITY BANK, SSB | 0107.01 | 50.00 |
| 2 | black | 41 | 72 | Denied | SECURITY BANK, SSB | 0108.01 | 50.00 |
| 3 | white | 42 | 75 | Loaned | SECURITY BANK, SSB | 0109.02 | 50.00 |
| 4 | black | 30 | 65 | Denied | SECURITY BANK, SSB | 0110.00 | 50.00 |
| 5 | white | 32 | 74 | Loaned | SECURITY BANK, SSB | 0115.00 | 50.00 |

Now you are ready to do crosstabs again. But you'll add one more element. Instead of having just two variables, "incrange" and "action," you'll also use "ethnic" in the third box. This additional variable allows you to separate out the income ranges and results into crosstabs for each ethnic group. This is known as "controlling" for ethnicity (see Table 6-33).

**TABLE 6-33**

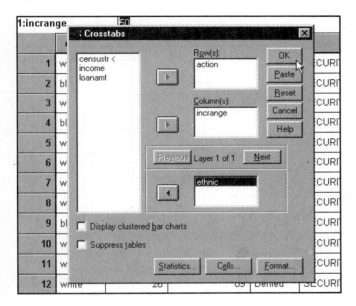

The results for blacks appear in Table 6-34.

**TABLE 6-34**

| Loan action * INCRANGE * ethnic Crosstabulation | | | | | | | | |
|---|---|---|---|---|---|---|---|---|
| | | | | | INCRANGE | | | |
| ethnic | | | | 25.00 | 50.00 | 75.00 | 100.00 | 1 |
| black | Loan action | Loaned | Count | 82 | 174 | 81 | 26 | |
| | | | % within INCRANGE | 36.1% | 43.4% | 52.3% | 61.9% | |
| | | Approved | Count | 17 | 27 | 18 | 2 | |
| | | | % within INCRANGE | 7.5% | 6.7% | 11.6% | 4.8% | |
| | | Denied | Count | 128 | 200 | 56 | 14 | |
| | | | % within INCRANGE | 56.4% | 49.9% | 36.1% | 33.3% | |
| | Total | | Count | 227 | 401 | 155 | 42 | |
| | | | % within INCRANGE | 100.0% | 100.0% | 100.0% | 100.0% | |

Now, focus on the applicants whose incomes range from $26,000 to $50,000 and from $51,000 to $75,000. Note that the denial rates are 49.9 and 36.1 percent, respectively. Then consider the results for whites, as shown in Table 6-35.

**TABLE 6-35**

| | | | INCRANGE | 100.0% | 100.0% | 100.0% | 100.0% |
|---|---|---|---|---|---|---|---|
| white | Loan action | Loaned | Count | 767 | 2351 | 1423 | 747 |
| | | | % within INCRANGE | 41.5% | 57.6% | 72.2% | 80.6% |
| | | Approved | Count | 209 | 435 | 184 | 78 |
| | | | % within INCRANGE | 11.3% | 10.7% | 9.3% | 8.4% |
| | | Denied | Count | 871 | 1293 | 364 | 102 |
| | | | % within INCRANGE | 47.2% | 31.7% | 18.5% | 11.0% |
| | Total | | Count | 1847 | 4079 | 1971 | 927 |
| | | | % within INCRANGE | 100.0% | 100.0% | 100.0% | 100.0% |

As you can see, the equivalent percentages for whites denied loans are 31.7 and 18.5 percent, respectively. The denial rates of blacks to whites in the middle class still range from 1.5 to 1, to 2 to 1. (That is, the ratio of 49.9 percent to 31.7 percent is 1.5 to 1, and 36.1 percent to 18.5 percent is nearly 2 to 1.)

At this point, you have established that blacks in the sample studied are denied loans more often than whites are, sometimes by a 2 to 1 ratio. That's a solid start for further inquiry.

Perhaps you might compare those applying for loans with the general population in the area. Or perhaps you should examine the reasons for denial. Was there a problem with creditworthiness, the total net worth of the applicants, or some other factor, such as location of the home?

You've now reached a point where the reporting really begins, and you are starting from much higher ground. Previously, you would have waited for a report and then done interviews. Now, you can write the rough draft of a report and begin a much more in-depth look at what is happening.

In the late 1980s, Bill Dedman won a Pulitzer Prize for the *Atlanta Journal-Constitution* with the help of computer-assisted reporting guru Dwight Morris, who supervised data analysis that revealed deep racial disparity in lending. In recent years, small and large news organizations have used the Home Mortgage database to raise questions about lending practices in their communities. In the mid-1990s, *U.S. News and World Report* conducted one of the most thorough studies ever done using this database.

Nonetheless, some social scientists and political conservatives have been highly critical of these kinds of initial analyses, saying that other factors—what Philip Meyer calls "lurking variables"—call into question the precision of the analyses and whether discrimination or bias actually occurs.

Lending institutions have not helped the situation, because the reasons for denials are usually not included in the database.

## Chapter Summary

❒ Although they are sometimes complex, basic statistics can help a journalist avoid pitfalls and carry out more sophisticated reporting.

❒ Mean, median, mode, and standard deviation are helpful when looking at databases.

❒ Frequencies allow a journalist to look quickly at a database to determine how many cases there are for different categories and what percentage of the total those cases represent.

❒ Crosstabs permit a journalist to study associations between different categories (or variables) to determine whether factors such as ethnicity are influencing decisions made by governments or businesses.

## Suggested Tasks

❒ Download from the World Wide Web or order from the National Institute for Computer-Assisted Reporting the sample home mortgage database used in this chapter.

❒ Use frequencies to determine how many applicants are in the database.

❐ Use descriptive statistics to find the average and standard deviation for the incomes and the amount of loan sought.

❐ Use the "Explore" part of the menu in SPSS to determine the median incomes and loan amounts for whites and blacks in the database.

❐ Use crosstabs to determine the percentage of blacks and whites denied loans.

❐ Use the "Recode" function to develop ranges of incomes.

❐ Use crosstabs to control for ethnicity and to compare the percentage of denials when incomes are similar.

# GETTING STORIES BY GOING ONLINE: SEARCHING, FINDING, AND DOWNLOADING

After terrorists bombed the federal building in Oklahoma City in April 1995, more journalists got on the Internet than ever before. There, they found information on rescue efforts, on survivors and victims, and on the investigation into the bombing. They discovered information on militia groups to which a suspect in the case was linked. And they located areas on the Internet where members of those groups discussed their philosophies.

Looking at information from the state of Oklahoma, the FBI, the Red Cross, newspapers, or other organizations, journalists could quickly discover details relating to the disaster. In fact, there were several online screens where journalists could begin searching for information, including the one shown in Table 7-1.

**TABLE 7-1**

| Location: | http://165.247.199.30./ |
|-----------|-------------------------|
| Welcome | What's New! | What's Cool! | Questions | Net Search | Net Direc |

## Welcome to the Internet Disaster Information Network

The Internet Disaster Information Network, provided as a public se
Internet Direct and Telekachina Productions, helps to distribu
news on disaster situations to the Internet community via the Worl

## Information on the bombing in Okla City:

At other online locations, the American Red Cross made announcements and requests, as shown in Table 7-2.

**TABLE 7-2**

Most extraordinary was that journalists were able to find these resources within half an hour by using the simplest tool on the Internet: the World Wide Web. Searching with tools such as WebCrawler, which looked like Table 7-3 at the time, and using the keyword "Oklahoma," journalists were able to hook into dozens of information areas known as "Web sites."

**TABLE 7-3**

The Internet (a loosely arranged network of computers around the world) has places for discussion groups (known as *listservs* and *newsgroups*); for files that can be read and transferred to your own computer (*file transfer protocol* or *FTP* sites); for computers that can be used for searching and data analysis (*Telnet* sites); and for sending messages via email. There also are tools, known by such names as *gopher* and *WAIS*, to search for files and for information within files.

The tools of the Internet and several online resources will be discussed briefly in this chapter. For example, many commercial online services not only provide a pathway to the Internet, but offer deep reservoirs of information. The America Online service and CompuServe, now owned by America Online, have archives of information on different subjects, particularly businesses. Infotek CDB and Autotrack offer extensive information on individuals, and Lexis-Nexis has an incredible collection of news stories. Such services, of course, charge a fee.

We will not go into the detail that other books do, but we will discuss the general resources and how some journalists have— or could have—used them. Furthermore, this handbook will not tell you how to hook up your computer or how to go online. There are people at your workplace or school who can do that for you. This handbook will attempt to provide only basic guidelines for reporting online and for gathering and downloading valuable databases, as well as tips for digging into the layers of information.

If you do need additional help, four publications come to mind immediately. A short, clear introductory book is Christopher Callahan's *A Journalist's Guide to the Internet* (1998). *The Online Student: Making the Grade on the Internet* (1995) by Randy Reddick and Elliot King is a step-by-step book for getting into online resources. *Online! A Reference Guide to Using Internet Sources* (1998) by Andrew Harnack and Eugene Kleppinger is also very good, and includes citation guidelines. And Nora Paul's *Computer Assisted Research*, <http://www.poynter.org/car/cg _chome.htm>, is a thorough online Web publication for journalists and librarians.

Note that by the time this book is published, the Internet and online resources may have undergone some changes and so the look of various screens also may have changed. But most of the principles of structure and searching will remain the same. And we can hope that one of the Internet's big advantages also will remain: except for initial online charges, much of it is free.

## ONLINE IN GENERAL

In 1991, before the Internet became a prevalent reporting tool, Michael Berens, then at the *Columbus Dispatch,* capped an intense phase of work in which he used online databases. Berens produced evidence that a serial killer was at work in several states and spurred law enforcement officials into action.

> HOT LINE ADDED TO KILLER SEARCH
>
> Attorney General Lee Fisher said yesterday an Ohio task force will use a national telephone hot line to collect tips in the slayings of 11 women who may be victims of a serial killer. He called it an unprecedented project.
>
> Fisher labeled the task force a "very high priority" and pledged financial support and manpower.
>
> In a series of articles since March 10, *The Dispatch* has detailed similarities in 11 slayings. The details had never been comprehensively compared because of a fragmented Ohio law enforcement system.[1]

As done during the *Hartford Courant*'s probe into possible serial killings in Connecticut (see Chapter 4), Berens, now at the *Chicago Tribune,* built his own database and used electronic information to link similar crimes committed in different locations at different times. But Berens's investigation was more far-ranging because the killer crossed state lines, murdering at truck stops along Interstate 70.

Relying on a hunch and a good reporter's instincts, Berens dialed into VuText, an online database at the time, to search and acquire electronic news clippings. Searching for the keywords "prostitute" and "body," he downloaded more than 60 stories. He

---

[1] Berens, M. Tracking a Hidden Serial Killer on the Interstate. *News Inc.* (April 1992), p. 18.

then culled pertinent details and put them into a spreadsheet, where he was able to analyze the similarities in certain murders.

Berens then wrote a series of news stories that culminated in the creation of the task force. With his straightforward approach, Berens demonstrated the incredible power of online resources.

Although some journalists are still puzzled about the practical use of online resources, many others have made use of them for daily stories and long-term projects. For example, Dave Davis and Ted Wendling at the *Plain Dealer* in Cleveland used online resources in 1992 to produce riveting stories about the perils of radiation treatment.[2] A Pulitzer Prize finalist, the series initially relied on an online database of the Nuclear Regulatory Commission called NUDOCS. A relentless search of the two million records in NUDOCS resulted in leads and details about people who had died from medical overdoses of radiation.

Nora Paul, head of library research at the Poynter Institute in St. Petersburg, Florida, constantly finds new resources and shares them with journalists. Kenton Robinson, a former projects editor and features writer at the *Hartford Courant* and now a book author, did not start a feature story without first conducting an online search. In those searches, he looked for experts, research papers, phone numbers, and discussion groups on the subject—whether it was tattoos or tall tales children tell each other.

"There is hardly a story I do that I don't use a modem," Robinson said. "It's like having a giant library–telephone directory at your desk, with information available to you almost instantaneously."[3]

*Newsday*'s Pulitzer Prize–winning coverage of the 1996 crash of TWA Flight 800 in the Atlantic waters off Long Island utilized online commercial databases, Web sites, newsgroups, and Federal Aviation Administration and National Transportation Safety Board online databases and reports. In the same year, the *Times-Picayune* in New Orleans subscribed to online fishery mailing lists to track issues and sources and to ask questions on a project about oceans, for which it also won a Pulitzer Prize.

---

[2] Davis, D., and Wendling, T. A. Deadly Cure. *Uplink* (February 1993), pp. 1–2.

[3] Robinson, K. Mining Your Manners Online. *Uplink* (June 1994), p. 2.

Admittedly, the world of online resources can sometimes be time-consuming, frustrating, and pointless. But if you approach that world with a plan and with an understanding of what findings are possible, you will reap rich results.

Overall, a journalist uses online databases for several purposes. Among them are:

☐ *Research.* A journalist can search through news clips, treatises, books, and other documents.

☐ *Interviews.* Online reporting allows a journalist to search for people such as experts, victims, and participants.

☐ *Analysis.* When a journalist finds a database that could be useful, he or she sometimes can use software to analyze it.

☐ *Database gathering.* A journalist can transfer (i.e., download) information to his or her own computer over phone lines or networks and then use a spreadsheet, database manager, or statistical or mapping software to analyze the information.

## ▮▤▤ WHAT'S OUT THERE AND WHAT CAN YOU USE?

What's out there? At first, too much.

One way to get on top of the online world is to think of it in two major forms: (1) traditional secondary resources, such as the costly archives of newspapers and lawsuits, and (2) nontraditional primary resources, such as government databases and discussion groups, that cost little or nothing.

The next question is, how can you trust what you find? Well, trust has nothing to do with information, electronic or otherwise. You need to verify and cross-reference whatever you find in the online world. You need to read up on what Web sites are reliable, and you need to know who has put them together. For example, Web sites with addresses ending in "gov" are constructed by government agencies and are generally as reliable as any government information.

The Internet as a whole can be as reliable (or unreliable) as going to an open city council meeting where irate citizens speak out, or as sitting in a restaurant and overhearing conversations.

As a good journalist, you would need to accurately identify the speaker, do a follow-up interview, and check out what was said. To blithely repeat what you hear never serves a journalist well.

## ▰▰▰ GETTING HELP FROM LIBRARY RESEARCHERS

Some journalists would rather rely on others to do their online work for them, and so they often go to experienced and professional online researchers.

Electronic library researchers (also known as *searchers*) are one of the first key resources for journalists heading online. Like traditional librarians, these researchers know where information is stored and how to find it. A library researcher should serve as a guide, providing invaluable advice and knowledge, helping with complex searches, and pointing journalists to the right resources.

Journalists need to learn how to go into the electronic stacks (1) to ask better questions when getting help from a researcher and (2) to do some of the research themselves. This is the same principle as using spreadsheets and database managers instead of relying on a data processor.

A good researcher thinks like a journalist, and a journalist can pick up insightful reporting techniques from a researcher. Many journalists are deft at interviewing primary resources, whether people or raw documents, but they avoid acquiring the researcher's skills to "interview" secondary sources such as articles, papers, books, or other studies. With both sets of skills, a journalist can go far by linking the library materials to interviews and tips.

## ▰▰▰ NEWSPAPER CLIPS

As Berens's work showed, an electronic library search of newspaper clips can turn up patterns and story tips. Several commercial services, such as Lexis-Nexis, provide this kind of resource. Lexis has legal documents, and Nexis has newspaper articles.

As a rule of thumb, every journalist should check the clips. For example, as far back as 1983, several reporters around the country got on the track of Long Island financier Mario Renda through the use of Lexis-Nexis. Renda's firm gave advice to pension fund managers, telling them where to put their funds for the best return on their money. Renda's firm received a fee for the advice. At the peak of his business in the early 1980s, his staff steered billions of dollars to banks and savings and loans throughout the country that offered the highest interest.

But there was a twist to Renda's operations that led to the failure of some of those financial institutions. Federal investigators have said that Renda's business associates told banks they could get pension funds only if they made loans to the associates for risky real estate deals. The banks, eager for huge pension deposits, made the loans—which were never repaid. Eventually, Renda was linked to the failure of more than a dozen banks in several states and was successfully prosecuted in federal court.

Federal investigators were not the first ones to uncover the complex scheme. Reporters and civil lawyers using Lexis-Nexis first linked Renda and his associates to banks and savings-and-loan problems. By searching databases of news clips and lawsuits, they found the money broker's name and his associates' names popping up in several states in connection with bank problems. From these simple searches, a pattern emerged.

In the preceding example, the power of online searching produced the picture of a serial killer of banks.

A search for anyone who has operated in several states should begin with these kinds of databases. The advantage is the scope of the information. The disadvantage is that lengthy searches can sometimes cost a lot.

## EMAIL

Email is often the means by which journalists first become comfortable with the online world. Using email is like sending and receiving letters, except that the letter appears on your computer screen instead of on paper in your mailbox. Email is also fast. It's so fast that people who use it call regular postal services "snail mail."

To send email, you need to know the email address of the person you want to contact. Online addresses can be almost cryptic. One of my email addresses used to be on CompuServe; it was <71023.120@CompuServe.com>. Not very illuminating, right?

At Investigative Reporters and Editors, Inc., where I work now, one of my addresses is <brant@ire.org>. A little more helpful, perhaps. If ever you need an address book, it's when you deal with email. In fact, most email services provide electronic address books.

Email is a good place to get comfortable online. You can use it to contact friends and family members, as well as experts and sources. Thus, it provides the initial satisfaction of making contact.

What's a practical use of email? Let's say you are looking for experts on health insurance. Send a message to ProfNet, which acts as an email distribution system. ProfNet, which is operated by PR Newswire, takes your email and sends it to public information officers at educational institutions. Those officers then contact experts on the subject, who reply to your query online or by phone or fax. Of course, you have to regard the experts with the same degree of skepticism you would have for any other source. Even so, ProfNet has proven itself to be a good resource for journalists.

First, you go to the Web site of ProfNet, at <www.profnet .com>, as shown in Table 7-4.

**TABLE 7-4**

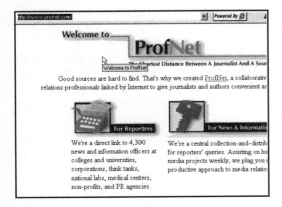

Then you click on the "For Reporters" box, and submit a query by filling out a submission form, the first part of which is shown in Table 7-5.

**TABLE 7-5**

Within hours, you would receive messages from afar. Naturally, you would have to follow up with phone calls and interviews—and determine how much an expert each "expert" is—but you could save a lot of time.

"Many reporters I talk to say they think using ProfNet is somehow cheating; it makes it too easy to find the right person to talk to," Robinson, formerly of the *Hartford Courant,* says. "But there is an art to the query, as it were. You must make it as precise (and concise) as possible and make clear how close your deadline looms."[4]

---

[4] Robinson, K. Mining Your Manners Online. *Uplink* (June 1994), p. 2.

## ▣▤ Listservs and Newsgroups

Another advantage of email is that you can send messages to hundreds or thousands of people at once. One way to do this is by joining *listserv* or a *newsgroup*. Messages sent to these locations can be read by everyone who has joined the listserv or visits that group.

You can join a listserv just by sending an email message to the person or institution that runs it. When I wanted to join the listserv of the National Institute for Computer-Assisted Reporting, I sent the message as shown in Table 7-6.

| **TABLE 7-6** |
| --- |
| To: listserv@lists.missouri.edu<br>Re: subscribe<br><br>subscribe nicar-l brant houston |

Once I joined this mailing list, I received messages in which people talked about how to do computer-assisted reporting. If you joined a listserv on environmental issues—as the *Times-Picayune* reporters did—or on military budgets, you would receive messages about those topics. You also could send messages to the listservs asking for help or information.

The problem with a listserv is that *all* the mail sent to that list is forwarded to your electronic mailbox, so you can end up getting more mail than you want. In addition, people do not always stick to the point and sometimes argue vigorously, which can become irritating.

If you don't want to receive all those messages, you might consider joining a newsgroup on the Internet instead. Newsgroups are like listservs, but you don't receive the messages in your mailbox. The messages are sent instead to a forum, where you can retrieve them. Newsgroup postings are somewhat like messages posted on a bulletin board.

One way to access a newsgroup is through the America Online service. If you click on "Internet" in the main menu, you get the screen shown in Table 7-7 (p. 134).

**TABLE 7-7**

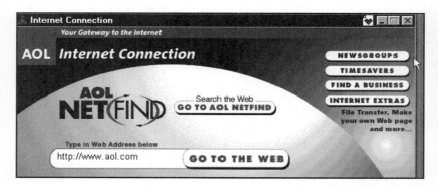

Similar screens exist on university networks and at businesses, but this one will work for demonstration purposes. Click on "Newsgroups" to bring up the screen shown in Table 7-8. Note the screen includes the term "Usenet," which is the network in which newsgroups exist.

**TABLE 7-8**

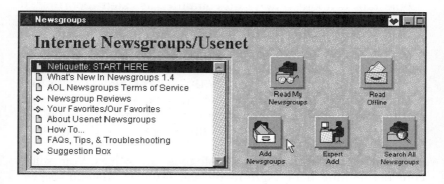

When you click on "Add Newsgroups," you will get a menu of categories, as shown in Table 7-9. In this case, we move down to "sci," because we're interested in planes and aeronautics and want to see what people are messaging about.

**TABLE 7-9**

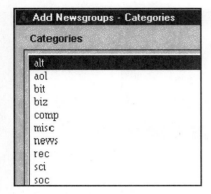

Clicking on "sci," we get a list of subcategories (Table 7-10). One of them is "sci.aeronautics."

**TABLE 7-10**

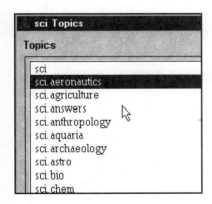

We click again and get another subgroup, "sci.aeronautics .airliners" (Table 7-11, p. 136).

**TABLE 7-11**

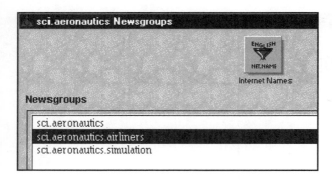

Now, by clicking on that group, we get a series of messages, some of which look intriguing, such as the potential fuel tank problem in 747s that was a concern of aviation safety officials looking into the crash of TWA Flight 800. (See Table 7-12.)

**TABLE 7-12**

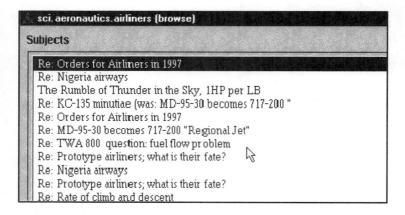

You can also search newsgroups without adding them. AltaVista, a Web search tool, allows you to search for subjects and issues within Usenet. (We'll talk more about search tools later in the chapter.) In Table 7-13, we are about to begin a search and type in the word "aeronautics."

**TABLE 7-13**

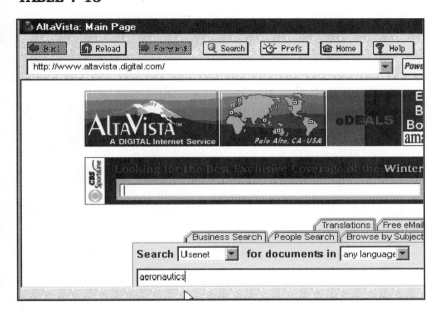

Another way to search is to go to the Web site of Deja News at <www.dejanews.com>, as shown in Table 7-14. Deja News keeps track of newsgroups and specializes in making it easy to find information.

**TABLE 7-14**

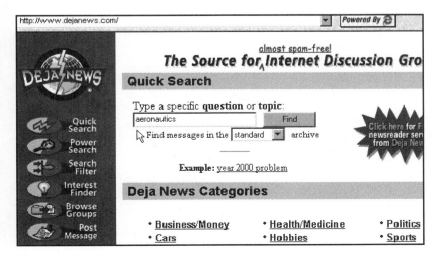

## ▉▬▬ SEARCHING THE WORLD WIDE WEB

Past the broad land of email lies the World Wide Web. For many journalists, the Web is still like a huge ocean or a landfill. You can fish valuable objects out of it, but often you have to troll for a long time or dig so deep that it doesn't seem worth it. Yet, every day, new tools are making Web searches much less arduous.

The Web is a friendly and efficient way of placing, finding, and linking to information on the Internet. Agencies, institutions, and businesses make information available through *homepages,* computer screens of text and colorful graphics that have addresses called *univeral resource locators,* or URLs. Furthermore, the Web carries not only data and text but also audio and video.

Another asset of the Web is that users can make their own "pages" and connections—or links—to other pages. By clicking on words or phrases highlighted in blue or another color on one homepage, a searcher can jump to other pages on other computers somewhere else in the world. The Web has effectively done for the Internet what Windows did for DOS operating systems on IBM-compatible computers. No longer do you need to type long commands. Instead, you move the cursor and click once, and you move to another site on the Internet.

To get around the Web, you need a "Web browser." A browser allows you to see graphics and connections and to link to search tools and indexes, such as Excite and Lycos, that help you find what you want. One of the most popular browsers is Netscape (Table 7-15) from Netscape Communications Corp. Another is Microsoft's Internet Explorer.

**TABLE 7-15**

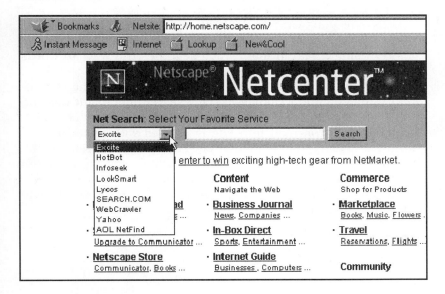

An extensive search area on Netscape (see Table 7-16) gives you ways to find information on issues, agencies, people, business, and many other subjects.

**TABLE 7-16**

| FEATURED SEARCHES | Amazon.com | AOL Buddies | Mu |
| --- | --- | --- |
| **SEARCH ENGINES** | **WEB GUIDES** | **WHITE & YELLOW PAGES** |
| AltaVista | AOL.com | BellSouth |
| AOL NetFind | Excite | Bigfoot |
| Electric Library: | Infoseek | Find a Business |
|   Research Archive | LookSmart | GTE SuperPages |
| HOTBOT | Lycos | WhoWhere? |
| WebCrawler | The Mining Co. | Yahoo! |

But how do you get to a destination (e.g., a database) if you don't have its address (the URL)?

Let's say you want to look at census data to determine whether your state's population has declined in recent years. Let's try using a search tool, which searches the Web for words or phrases that you have specified.

Search tools and guides are like librarians—each one has different strengths and weaknesses. One search tool might not find what you are looking for, but perhaps another one will. Furthermore, if the road to a site is clogged with digital traffic, you can always try to find another path using another search tool.

Using the popular search tool AltaVista, let's try a search with the words "census bureau state+population+estimates." (See Table 7-17.) The "+" sign guarantees those words will appear in the documents matched.

**TABLE 7-17**

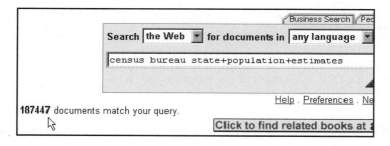

As you can see, there is a problem. The search tool has found 187,447 documents, which, even prioritized, isn't going to work.

So, in Table 7-18, we narrow our search, requiring that all the keywords are in the criteria for a search.

**TABLE 7-18**

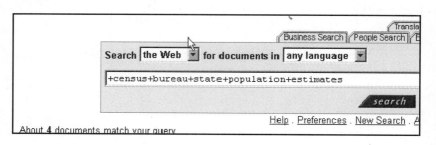

This time, we get fewer documents. In Table 7-19, we scan down and click on our choice, "State Population Estimates."

**TABLE 7-19**

3. State Population Estimates
STATE POPULATION ESTIMATES. 1990 to 1996 Annual Time Series of State F
Includes: U.S., Regions, Divisions, and States. 1995-96...
*http://www.census.gov/population/www/estimates/statepop.html* - *size 7K - 5-*

When we click on the choice, it links us directly to the pages of the U.S. Census Bureau. Now we can choose the database we want and click on it (see Table 7-20).

**TABLE 7-20**

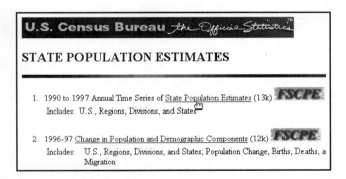

This gives us the information we need on population changes in regions and states, as shown in Table 7-21.

**TABLE 7-21**

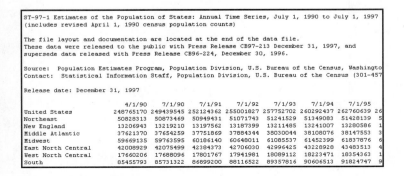

| | 4/1/90 | 7/1/90 | 7/1/91 | 7/1/92 | 7/1/93 | 7/1/94 | 7/1/95 | |
|---|---|---|---|---|---|---|---|---|
| United States | 248765170 | 249439545 | 252124362 | 255001827 | 257752702 | 260292437 | 262760639 | 26 |
| Northeast | 50828313 | 50873469 | 50949431 | 51071743 | 51241529 | 51349083 | 51428139 | 5 |
| New England | 13206943 | 13219210 | 13197562 | 13187399 | 13211485 | 13241007 | 13280586 | 1 |
| Middle Atlantic | 37621370 | 37654259 | 37751869 | 37884344 | 38030044 | 38108076 | 38147553 | 3 |
| Midwest | 59669135 | 59763595 | 60186140 | 60648011 | 61085537 | 61452399 | 61837876 | 6 |
| East North Central | 42008929 | 42075499 | 42384373 | 42706030 | 42996425 | 43228928 | 43483513 | 4 |
| West North Central | 17660206 | 17688096 | 17801767 | 17941981 | 18089112 | 18223471 | 18354363 | 1 |
| South | 85455793 | 85731322 | 86899200 | 88116522 | 89357816 | 90606513 | 91824747 | 9 |

We can save this information by clicking on "File" at the top of the screen, clicking on "Save as," and saving the data as a text file (Table 7-22).

**TABLE 7-22**

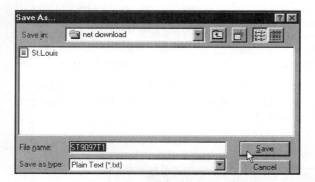

Some Web sites are gateways to other Web sites. FedWorld, for example, provides access and direction to other federal agency sites. FedWorld is generally easy to get to and is growing every day in size and scope. Table 7-23 shows the FedWorld homepage.

**TABLE 7-23**

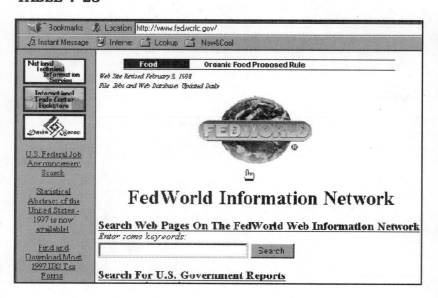

When you first go to a new page, you will need to type in the long address—in this case, <www.fedworld.com>—but you can then save it under "Bookmark" so you'll never have to type it again. (Journalists constantly save favorite locations, thereby saving each other time in doing searches.)

We will use a link FedWorld has in order to pursue our inquiry about TWA Flight 800 and problems with fuel tanks. (See Table 7-24.)

**TABLE 7-24**

This link, "Locate Important FAA Documents," takes us to a screen where we can perform a search for information within FAA documents and reports. (See Table 7-25.)

**TABLE 7-25**

With this search, we get results quickly (Table 7-26).

**TABLE 7-26**

| | FAA Document Archive Search Results |
|---|---|
| 1 | AD97--26.LRG 15K 01/07/97 96-26-52 BOEING 747 |
| 2 | AD97--28.LRG 21K 01/08/97 96-26-06 BOEING 747 |
| 3 | AD97--33.LRG 13K 01/09/97 96-26-51 BOEING 747 |
| 4 | AD97--85.LRG 19K 02/13/97 97-03-19 BOEING 747 |
| 5 | AD97--24.LRG 13K 01/03/97 96-26-04 BOEING 747 |
| 6 | AD97-178.LRG 18K 05/05/97 97-09-13 BOEING 747 |
| 7 | AD97-323.LRG 16K 09/24/97 97-20-01 BOEING 747 |

Within moments, by checking out the selections, we come upon the airworthiness directive—AD97-28.LRG—put out by the FAA on possible fuel tank problems in the Boeing 747 that are suspected in the Flight 800 crash. (See Table 7-27.)

**TABLE 7-27**

```
Airworthiness Directives; Boeing Model 747 Series Airplanes

AGENCY:  Federal Aviation Administration, DOT.

ACTION:  Final rule; request for comments.

SUMMARY:  This amendment adopts a new airworthiness
directive (AD) that is applicable to certain Boeing Model
747 series airplanes. This action requires a one-time
inspection to detect damage of the sleeving and wire bundles
of the boost pumps of the numbers 1 and 4 main fuel tanks,
and of the auxiliary tank jettison pumps (if installed);
replacement of any damaged sleeving with new sleeving; and
repair or replacement of any damaged wires with new wires.
```

If you wanted to, you could save the entire text of the directive by highlighting the text and saving it as a text file.

## ■■■ FILE TRANSFER PROTOCOL:
## A WAY TO DOWNLOAD BIG DATABASES

Sometimes, the information or database that you want from the Web is too large for easy copying. At that point, you will want to use FTP, or *file transfer protocol.* The basic concept of FTP is that a government agency or organization stores databases in an electronic warehouse where you can go and digitally cart them out.

Here's a quick example: The Campaign Finance Information Center's Web site at <www.campaignfinance.org> offers information about state and local political campaigns, usually compiled by independent groups. (See Table 7-28.)

**TABLE 7-28**

Once you have accessed their homepage, clicking on "The CFIC Data Center" under "Databases" gives you access to campaign finance databases for states all over the country. Table 7-29 (p. 146) shows the database for Illinois.

**TABLE 7-29**

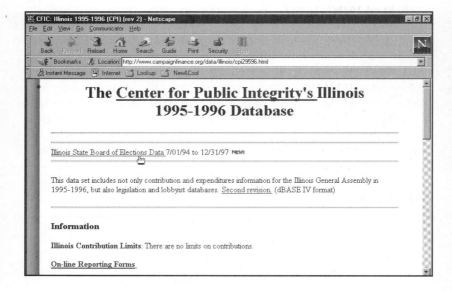

As you can see, you did not need to know a special program or program language to undertake your search. Instead, you essentially went on a treasure hunt that involved moving the cursor onto a shaded word and clicking to find the next clue.

## STATE GOVERNMENTAL DATABASES

Many state governments and municipal agencies are also placing information on the Web at a surprising rate. They have discovered that having Web pages saves both time and money spent on the telephone.

Even before the advent of the Web, news organizations in New Mexico, Florida, New York, Ohio, Connecticut, and other states had obtained access to state government databases, including civil and criminal court records, county records, and city records. For example, Rose Ciotta, former computer-assisted reporting editor at the *Buffalo News*, was able to tap into city databases online through an old-fashioned modem-to-modem arrangement and do searches and queries.

One example of how access to court records can save time is the way in which the *Hartford Courant* checked state civil court records during the downfall of a billion-dollar real estate empire. In this case, there were more than a dozen courthouses throughout the state, and unhappy investors were filing civil suits against the real estate company every day. George Gombossy, the lead reporter on the story, could not have kept up with the filings without a team of colleagues rushing around the state each afternoon. But, because the *Courant* could tap into the civil-court electronic docket online, Gombossy could check all the courthouses in a half hour for lawsuits and decide which ones were worth investigating.

It is becoming so routine for states to place information on the Web that you can find information from every state in the nation. (The Campaign Finance Information Center, which is run by Investigative Reporters and Editors, has cataloged and linked state freedom-of-information and election sites.)

As a result of the proliferation of state data on the Web, a disparity often exists between what an agency will give out to a reporter in person and what that reporter can get from the Web.

At the Missouri School of Journalism, a student in one of my classes was working on a ground contamination story. He asked the Missouri Department of Natural Resources for a database on the location of underground petroleum storage tanks that might be leaking. After weeks of requests, he still had no database. At that point, we decided to tour the agency's Web site in the hope that the agency had placed the information there.

Within a short time, we had located the Division of Environmental Quality online, as shown in Table 7-30.

**TABLE 7-30**

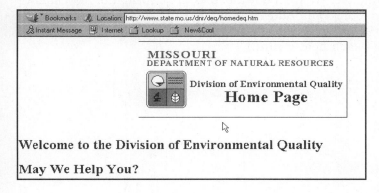

Next, we looked for links to a page on hazardous sites and found the list shown in Table 7-31.

**TABLE 7-31**

Administration
- Air Pollution Control Program
- Environmental Service Program (Laboratory)
- Hazardous Waste Program
- Land Reclamation Program
- Public Drinking Water Program
- Regional Offices
- Soil and Water Conservation Program
- Solid Waste Management Program
- Technical Assistance Program
- Water Pollution Control Program

We clicked on "Hazardous Waste Program" and found a free "File Download Page" of databases, as shown in Table 7-32.

**TABLE 7-32**

- Graphics Portraying Hazardous Waste Management In Missouri
- Frequently Requested Phone Numbers
- Hazardous Waste Management Commission
- Program Functions
- Regional Office Activities
- Technical Bulletins and Fact Sheets
- Commercial Hazardous Waste Facilities Located In Missouri
- File Download Page

Among the free downloads, we found the petroleum storage tank database. We then downloaded the information by clicking on "Petroleum Tank Address File" in Table 7-33. (We also downloaded the two other files, a related database and a text file that told what each field meant.)

**TABLE 7-33**

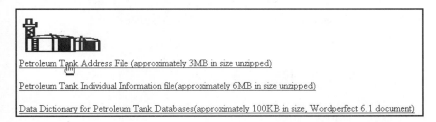

Petroleum Tank Address File (approximately 3MB in size unzipped)

Petroleum Tank Individual Information file(approximately 6MB in size unzipped)

Data Dictionary for Petroleum Tank Databases(approximately 100KB in size, Wordperfect 6.1 document)

When we clicked to download, we got the window shown in Table 7-34 and chose "Save File."

**TABLE 7-34**

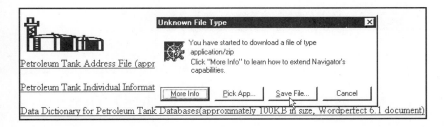

When we chose "Save File," we chose the folder to download it in, as shown in Table 7-35.

**TABLE 7-35**

| Save As... | ? ✕ |
|---|---|
| Save in: | 📁 net download |

| File name: | fac_net | Save |
|---|---|---|
| Save as type: | All Files (*.*) | Cancel |

When we chose "Save," the file took only a few minutes to download to our computer (see Table 7-36), and weeks of frustration were overcome in less than half an hour.

**TABLE 7-36**

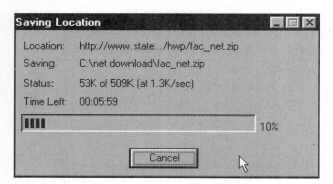

We later opened the file in Microsoft Access, and there were the street addresses for storage tanks—exactly what the student needed to get a handle on the story. (These addresses were the ones used to map the sites of the petroleum tanks in Chapter 5.)

These short examples show the incredible value of the Web and how easily it allows us to use many of the tools of computer-assisted reporting to begin stories at a high level. In this new world of journalism, we can search countless electronic libraries, find reports, discover discussion groups, and do research for any story imaginable.

## CHAPTER SUMMARY

❐ The Internet has become easier to understand, and much of it is still free.

❐ You can receive email and join discussion groups through listservs and newsgroups.

❐ Many search tools exist to help you locate information online.

❐ Online resources allow you to research stories quickly and effectively.

❐ Using only a keyword or two, you can search news clips to find the subject in which you are interested.

❐ You can use email to contact experts.

❐ You can use commercial online resources to look up phone numbers, join discussion groups, and research the background of people and businesses.

## ▪▦ SUGGESTED TASKS

❐ Use three different search tools to look for information on the same subject. (Read their "Help" files.)

❐ Join two listservs.

❐ Use a search tool to research newsgroup discussions.

❐ Download several small databases from government agencies.

❐ Research a prominent politician through the Web.

# OBTAINING DATABASES:
# LOCATING, NEGOTIATING, AND IMPORTING

In 1992, using a wealth of electronic information, the *National Law Journal* did a precedent-setting story that showed how minority communities in the United States had become dumping grounds for hazardous pollutants. But finding the right databases for the story was not easy. The first disk that the reporters obtained on cleaning up dangerous Superfund sites was flawed: it did not indicate when the sites were cleaned up or what occurred after a site was identified.

Federal Environmental Protection Agency (EPA) officials initially denied that such information existed. Then, when they admitted it did exist, they wanted to charge thousands of dollars for access. By working sources, Marianne Lavelle, a *Law Journal* reporter, persuaded one lone EPA officer to supply a disk at no charge. "It wasn't through FOIA [Freedom of Information Act] requests but through reporting skills and a reasonable EPA officer that we were able to obtain the data we needed," said Lavelle.

Then the reporters circumvented a commercial vendor who wanted to sell them data at a high charge—they went instead to a nonprofit organization that sold the same data for much less. The reporters also obtained civil court data through other agencies when the EPA refused to give them access to it.[1]

---

[1] Devine, K. The National Law Journal Uncovers Injustice in Environmental Cleanup. *Uplink* (April/May 1993), p. 4.

**152**

Sometimes, the database you need is freely and openly distributed. At other times, you have to dig, argue, and push to get what should be public information.

This chapter will look at the three steps for obtaining access to databases: finding, negotiating, and importing.

**1.** You need to *find out* what the right database for the story is and what information within it you really need.

**2.** You often need to *negotiate* knowledgeably for the database, avoiding stonewalling by bureaucrats who try to snow you with technical terms and acquiring the supplementary material necessary to understand the database.

**3.** You need to know how to *import,* or transfer, the data from a diskette or other media source so that you can use it.

A free and democratic society is based on openness, not bureaucracy. In seeking electronic information, remember that the keeper of public information should have to give you a good reason not to release the information. You should not have to give the agency head a good reason to release it. Taxpayers have already supplied the money to enter the data, store the data, and retrieve the data. In short, you need to think: "You have it. I want it. Give it to me."

## ▮▀ FINDING DATA

Many journalists starting out in computer-assisted reporting wonder where they can find useful databases. The answer is: "everywhere."

There are databases on almost any subject and at almost any agency. Since the rise of personal computers, most governmental agencies and businesses have been storing their information electronically. Only journalists and old-fashioned town clerks have been particularly slow to change from the paper world to the digital.

For example, the Federal Data Base Finder, which is available on CD-ROM for less than $60 as well as online, lists thousands of federal databases. A sample listing from the CD-ROM is given in Table 8-1.

**TABLE 8-1**

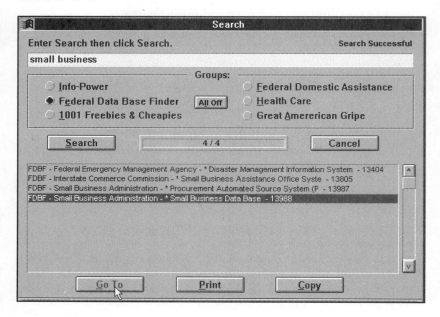

When you type "small business" in the "Search" area, you can quickly search hundreds of database listings for any mention of small business. By moving the cursor from the first down to the fourth listing at the bottom of the screen, clicking there, and hitting "Go To," you can get the information shown in Table 8-2.

**TABLE 8-2**

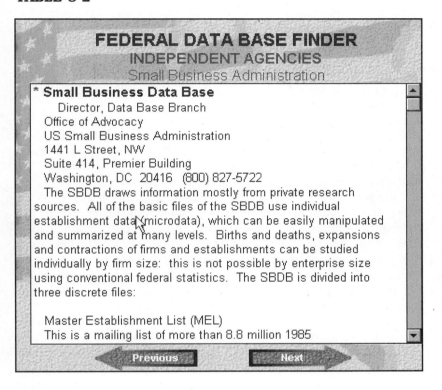

FEDERAL DATA BASE FINDER
INDEPENDENT AGENCIES
Small Business Administration

\* **Small Business Data Base**
   Director, Data Base Branch
   Office of Advocacy
   US Small Business Administration
   1441 L Street, NW
   Suite 414, Premier Building
   Washington, DC 20416   (800) 827-5722
   The SBDB draws information mostly from private research
   sources. All of the basic files of the SBDB use individual
   establishment data (microdata), which can be easily manipulated
   and summarized at many levels. Births and deaths, expansions
   and contractions of firms and establishments can be studied
   individually by firm size: this is not possible by enterprise size
   using conventional federal statistics. The SBDB is divided into
   three discrete files:

   Master Establishment List (MEL)
   This is a mailing list of more than 8.8 million 1985

[Previous]   [Next]

Each entry in the Federal Data Base Finder gives a phone
number and a description of a file. The Federal Data Base
Finder also will lead you to unexpected places. For example, a
search on the word *health* might turn up many entries from the
Department of Agriculture.

As CD-ROMs have become more popular, there are more
databases of databases. There is a hard-copy version of available state databases that is not as complete as the Federal Data
Base Finder, but it is useful nonetheless. Individual states or
vendors are moving ahead on listing databases, either in
reports or online. Florida puts out a list of state databases in
electronic form.

Even without these guides on a state level, you'll still find that most departments are computerized and have extensive databases. When you walk into a state office, look around and you'll see everyone typing information into computers. At a city or town hall, you'll see the same thing, whether you are at the building inspector's office or the registrar of deeds, where real estate records are kept.

If there is a printout, there generally is a database. It's surprising how many times reporters return to a newsroom saying that an agency has told them there is no electronic information. The reporters say the agency only had "this," holding up a printout. In fact, it's nearly impossible to print out information if it's not already in some kind of usable electronic format.

Furthermore, if there is a report in a pamphlet or booklet, there is probably one or more databases behind it. State and federal housing agencies often issue reports about where subsidized housing is located, how many units are at that location, and who can qualify for the housing. By asking for the backup electronic information on such a report, a reporter can obtain not only the columns and rows that appear in the report, but also material that might have been excluded from it.

Some states (Iowa, for example) require agencies to provide a list of databases. But in other states, many agencies may say that a database doesn't exist because they don't want to be bothered with granting your request or because they have something to hide. But these same agencies may have hired a consultant to unravel the mess they made of their computer systems over the past two decades. The consultant issues reports, which include inventories of hardware, software, and databases. These reports can serve as an index when you are trying to determine whether an agency has what you need. Ask the agency for copies of consultant reports on its computer systems.

Auditors' reports also generally contain an overview of an agency's records and how they are kept. The General Accounting Office, a congressional watchdog, often uses an agency's own databases to perform its audits. The databases are described in the back of the GAO reports. And as we saw in the previous chapter, you can obtain summaries of these reports online.

In addition, governmental bulletin boards are good sources for finding data. Although the databases themselves may not be available online, reports, summaries, and discussions of these databases are mentioned.

The Federal Aviation Administration's Web site (discussed in Chapter 7) provides a guide to its own databases in its list of records available.

You can also look through commercial and governmental database catalogs. The catalog put out by the commercial Dialog service lists databases you may have never thought of. In some cases, an agency staff member may be unaware of the agency's databases, but the database is listed in the National Technical Information Services (NTIS) catalog. The *National Law Journal* reporters mentioned at the beginning of this chapter used NTIS diskettes of EPA databases when the EPA refused to release them. Many agencies actually depend on NTIS to distribute their information.

Getting onto bulletin boards and listservs on the Internet and simply asking if a database exists is also a good approach.

In addition, developing sources among social scientists at universities and colleges can open up wide avenues of database possibilities. These social researchers live in a world of data-bases, because they rely on data for their statistical analyses.

If you cover a beat, you should develop sources at three or more levels. First, talk to data-entry clerks; they have few politics to play, and they can tell you what kind of information they are entering. Second, talk to data processors; they can tell you what kind of information they are processing. Third, talk to administrators; they can tell you what kind of information they use for the reports they issue.

There are also associations you should know about or join. People who belong to groups that use SAS or SPSS know about a wide range of data, from hospitals to insurance to government. The Association for Public Data Users (APDU) puts out a monthly newsletter that discusses public data. Membership in the APDU costs several hundred dollars a year, but it's worth it. Perhaps you can get your company to pay.

## ▉▤▤ OBTAINING A DATABASE

The first way to obtain a database is to ask for it. Do not write a formal request under the Freedom of Information Act. Just ask.

Some reporters keep blank disks with them. If they find a database at an agency, they pull out a disk and ask to copy the data right away. You would be surprised how often they get databases this way. In fact, Bob Port, formerly with the *St. Petersburg Times* and now with the Associated Press, went from carrying a portable copier to carrying a portable computer tape drive when he visited agencies in Florida.

To obtain a database, you generally need to know what to ask for. You also need to know the laws and regulations governing the release of electronic information, but not necessarily to use them as leverage. In fact, sometimes you need to know not to bring them up. Many state laws are so antiquated or so confusing that they can effectively block the release of information. The Reporters Committee for Freedom of the Press puts out a booklet, *Access to Electronic Records,* that summarizes the states' laws and gives advice on obtaining electronic information.[2] They also have a Web site: <www.rcfp.org>.

## ▉▤▤ WHAT PARTICULAR INFORMATION DO YOU NEED?

Before you begin a fight for information, make sure you know what you want. Conversely, know what you can give up. If you only need zip codes for your story, don't argue over street addresses.

You need to know how the information is kept. Is it on a personal computer? Is it on a mainframe? Is it in a spreadsheet or database manager, or in some ancient programming language? In what kind of format can the agency give it to you? What does the record layout look like? How many megabytes is the file?

If the information is on a personal computer, it will probably be easy to obtain in a usable form. If the information is on a

---

[2] Reporters Committee for Freedom of the Press. *Access to Electronic Records* (fall 1994). Updated regularly.

mainframe computer, you need to know whether the agency can copy the information onto diskettes or only onto a computer tape. For computer tape, you'll need to have access to another mainframe or a portable tape drive reader.

If the information is on IBM-compatible or Macintosh software, you will be able to handle it. But if it comes to you with weird programming characters, it may be more trouble than it's worth.

If the database is 200 megabytes and your hard drive is 100 megabytes, you will need to reconsider your request, reduce your request, or find a bigger hard drive. And like buying a car, you need to know what a fair price is and what you are willing to pay. You also will be forced into learning some technospeak.

## ▮▅▅ RECORD LAYOUT

If the information is in a spreadsheet on a disk, you have a good chance of not needing to know too much about the record layout. With modern spreadsheets, you generally get the disk, copy information from the disk to your hard drive, and open the file, and your own spreadsheet puts the information on the spreadsheet grid.

That's the easy way.

Most of the time, however, you will get information that has been kept in a database manager. In Chapter 4, we discussed record layout and database managers. A record layout serves as a guide to how the information is stored and ordered. The record layout specifies:

❐  The name of each column (a "field").

❐  Whether it's a field that is alphanumeric (consisting of letters and numbers), numeric (only numbers), or dates.

❐  How wide each field is. A field can contain only so many characters or numbers, depending on its width. (It's like filling out test forms that give you only 12 spaces for your last name. If your last name is Rumpelstiltskin, only "Rumpelstilts" will fit.)

❒ The position of the field in the record. If a record is 100 characters long and the last-name field is the first field, then the last-name field's position is 1–12. Think of a record as a linear crossword puzzle.

Before you acquire a database, it's wise to get the record layout first. The record layout will tell you what information is in the database and whether it fits your needs. You may need some explanation of the categories of information, because sometimes they are abbreviated in military style (i.e., with acronyms). For example, you may find the category "CANDID." This does not mean "candid"; it means "*cand*idate *id*entification number." Table 8-3 shows a modified record layout for individual contributors to federal political campaigns.

| TABLE 8-3 | | |
|---|---|---|
| RECIPID | Character | 9 |
| AMENDMENT | Character | 1 |
| REPORT | Character | 3 |
| PRIMGEN | Character | 1 |
| MICROFILM | Character | 11 |
| CONTTYPE | Character | 3 |
| NAME | Character | 50 |
| CITY | Character | 18 |
| STATE | Character | 2 |
| ZIP | Character | 5 |
| OCCUPATION | Character | 35 |
| CONTDATE | Date | 8 |
| AMOUNT | Numeric | 7 |
| OTHERID | Character | 9 |
| COMMCODE | Character | 1 |
| CANDID | Character | 9 |

As you can see, the field names are somewhat cryptic, and most field types are character instead of alphanumeric. You can also see that the record length—if you add up all the fields—is 172 spaces. If you knew you were getting 10,000 records, you could calculate how big the file is. Multiply 172 by 10,000, and you get 1,720,000 bytes, or about 1.7 megabytes.

In addition, you will need the record layout if you are going to import the information into your own database manager software. By "import," we mean that you will transfer the information into your own database while translating it (if necessary) into the database manager language.

You also should obtain the codebook or code sheet that goes with the data, if there is one. Why? Because to save time and space, a database maker does not write, for example, "black," "white," or "Hispanic." Instead, the database maker designs the ethnicity column to have only one character, coding blacks as "1," whites as "2," and Hispanics as "3." Although you might be able to figure out some codes on your own, it's not a good idea to get into a guessing game. So obtain the codebook or the code sheet.

You should also get a printout of the first 10 to 100 records. (What? you ask. I thought I shouldn't get printouts.) Well, always get a printout so you can see whether information has been entered into all the fields. You also need the printout to make sure that you have transferred the information properly into your computer. Also, get a hard copy of the form from which the information was entered. This is known as an *integrity check*, which will be covered in more detail in Chapter 9.

## ▰▰▰ COMPUTER TAPES

Governmental agencies and private businesses are slowly replacing nine-track computer tapes with smaller tapes, CD-ROMs, and other forms of storage. The nine-track tape is the large reel of magnetic tape shown in the background of computer rooms in science-fiction movies. The tapes can be fragile and hard to deal with.

If a database is delivered on a nine-track tape, you will need more than the record layout. You will need to know the following:

❏ *The language, or code, the information is in.* EBCDIC or ASCII is the choice. (EBCDIC, pronounced "Ebb-See-Dic," stands for Extended Binary Coded Decimal Interchange Code. ASCII—"Ask-key"—stands for American Standard

Code for Information Interchange.) A personal computer reads ASCII; if the tape is in EBCDIC (which it will be if it comes from an IBM mainframe), you will have to translate it into ASCII. Don't worry; there are a lot of programs that do this. Many journalists use Nine-Track Express, which can be obtained from the National Institute for Computer-Assisted Reporting.

❏ *The format.* Generally, you should ask for "fixed format," which means that all the information can be easily imported into a database manager. ASCII "comma delimited" format is also acceptable.

❏ *The density of the tape.* Density means the number of bits that are squeezed onto eight of the nine tracks on the tape (remember that 8 bits make up a byte). The ninth track is used for checking the data.

Most tapes come in 1,600 or 6,250 bits per inch (bpi). Tapes using 6,250 bpi, of course, hold much more information: a total of 120 megabytes or more per track. A 6,250-bpi tape will cut down on cost because it means using fewer tapes. So you want 6,250 bpi.

❏ *The blocking factor.* To get more information on a tape, records are squeezed into blocks. If records are 100 bytes long and have a blocking factor of 10, then there are 1,000 bytes in each block. If the blocking factor is 20, then each block holds 2,000 bytes. Use this formula when you want to determine whether an agency gave you the right specifications.

Table 8-4 presents some typical tape specifications information.

| TABLE 8-4 | |
|---|---|
| Density | 6250 bpi |
| Format | Fixed |
| Record length | 100 |
| Blocking factor | 10 |
| Block size | 1000 |
| Coding | EBCDIC |
| Number of records | 851,777 |

To review, if you are given a disk, you need to ask for a record layout, a code sheet printout of the first 10 records, and the language the database is in.

If you are given a computer tape, you also need to ask the following:

❐ What language is it in? ASCII or EBCDIC?
❐ What is the format? Fixed or other?
❐ What is the density? 6,250 bpi or other?
❐ What is the record length?
❐ What is the blocking factor?
❐ How many records will I receive?

The most thorough and easiest-to-understand manual for journalists using computer tapes is the one that accompanies Nine-Track Express, the software written for transferring data from tapes to hard drives. The software was written by two pioneers in computer-assisted reporting, Elliot Jaspin and Daniel Woods.

## PRIVACY

Jennifer LaFleur, the former training director for the National Institute for Computer-Assisted Reporting, was driving to a seminar in Los Angeles when she saw a sign proclaiming that the next two miles of highway were sponsored by singer-actress Bette Midler. LaFleur thought that in an area where so many celebrities live, a story about such sponsorships would make good reading. When she called the California Highway Department, however, she learned that although an Adopt-A-Highway electronic database existed, under California law the information on the names was private—even though the names were on billboards! This is the kind of absurd world you may enter when trying to obtain data.

If an agency claims that its information is private, check the laws and regulations. If the agency is right, decide whether the rest of the information is still valuable. In the Adopt-A-Highway example, it was worthless to get the database without the names because the names were the point of the story.

Many reporters, by knowing what they need for a story, can agree to the deletion of certain categories. For example, the name field is unnecessary when you're using a database for a demographic or statistical study. Reporters often give up names on medical or workers' compensation records because there are a generous number of cases in open civil court that can be used for anecdotes. If you are seeking state employee records, there are many stories you can do without getting street addresses. Rather than enter into a year-long debate, you can give up some fields in exchange for the rest and still get the story.

## ▪▬▬ HIGH COSTS

Several newspapers have been asked to pay millions of dollars when their reporters sought information. Often, the final cost has been a few hundred dollars or less. Over the years, the *Boston Herald* sought driver's license records from the state of Massachusetts. The state first asked for $168,000, but it eventually sold the records for $77. The state of Connecticut first asked the *Hartford Courant* for $3 million for the same kind of records. Three years later, after long negotiations, the *Courant* paid a dollar. Texas reporters were asked for $45 million.

You can prevail if you are willing to haggle and if you know what a fair price should be. Here are three guidelines:

❏ *The cost of the media.* A diskette costs less than a dollar, a computer tape less than $20, and a CD-ROM less than $5.

❏ *The cost of copying.* An agency should not charge you for copying information from the hard drive of a personal computer to a few disks. The cost of copying from a mainframe to a computer tape or disk should cost only a few dollars for "runtime."

❏ *The cost of staff time.* Generally, the public has already paid for the collection and storage of data. Unless you ask for special programming, an agency should be hard-pressed to charge you for programming. If it does, the cost should not be more than $20 to $30 an hour. You should avoid programming wherever possible, because it means errors can be made, and it gives the agency one more chance to take out records that might lead to an embarrassing story.

In practical terms, you should be able to obtain most databases for $100 or less. Even in those cases, you should ask for a fee waiver, because disclosure of this information is in the public's interest. (As mentioned previously, the taxpayers have already paid for data entry, storage, and retrieval of the information.)

One threat to the open use of electronic records is the handling of public records by private vendors. Public agencies that don't have computer expertise often hire commercial vendors to do the work for them. But commercial vendors want to make a profit. If a citizen asks for the information, some commercial vendors will charge prohibitive fees.

You may be able to circumvent this problem by asking the agency to give you a copy of its on-site files. However, many agencies don't have a copy of their own records. You then have to argue with the commercial vendor. Your best solution is to get the law changed. In some states, it is illegal for commercial vendors to charge exorbitant prices for public information.

## ■▬▬ IMPORTING DATABASES

You don't want to go through all the work of obtaining a database and then not be able to use it. That's why it's important to get the record layout, size of the file, code sheet, and printout. (*Note:* This book won't cover the importing of computer tapes, although many concepts used for importing from disks to hard drives are the same as those for importing from computer tapes to hard drives.)

There are two key aspects of importing. One, make sure that the information goes into the correct columns and that those columns are labeled correctly. Two, make sure that the information is properly translated so you can read it.

If you receive the information in one of the common database software languages, your job will be straightforward.

Different databases previously tried not to translate the database software of other companies, but now they do. As an example, if you are importing a Microsoft Excel or dBASE III file into Access (see "Files of type" field in Table 8-5), you need only identify the original program, and the information will automatically be loaded into Access. This is illustrated in Table 8-5. Other types of files on the menu in Table 8-5 are text files and HTML documents.

**TABLE 8-5**

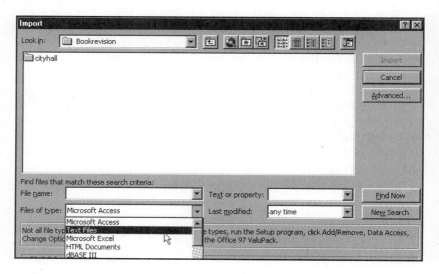

Note there are many kinds of software that Access can translate.

Sometimes, you will receive information in ASCII, the common language of personal computers. ASCII files come in "fixed format" and "comma delimited." Fixed format is shown in Table 8-6.

**TABLE 8-6**

```
Candidate                    Contribution  Donor
CLINTON, WILLIAM JEFFERSON       250ABRAMSON, LYNN
CLINTON, WILLIAM JEFFERSON      1000ACKERMAN, BRUCE
CLINTON, WILLIAM JEFFERSON      1000ACORN, DAVID P
DOLE, ROBERT J                  1000ADAMS, JENNIFER L
DOLE, ROBERT J                  -500ADAMS, JENNIFER L
DOLE, ROBERT J                  1000ADAMS, JOHN E
CLINTON, WILLIAM JEFFERSON       250ADAMS, ROBERT M
CLINTON, WILLIAM JEFFERSON       250AKINS, PAMELA S
CLINTON, WILLIAM JEFFERSON       250AKINS, PAMELA S
CLINTON, WILLIAM JEFFERSON      1000ALBERT, JANET
CLINTON, WILLIAM JEFFERSON      1000ALBERT, JOEL S
DOLE, ROBERT J                   250ALFANO, CHARLES E
DOLE, ROBERT J                   500ALFANO, SUSAN A
DOLE, ROBERT J                  -250ALFANO, SUSAN A
CLINTON, WILLIAM JEFFERSON       250ALIC, ANITA M
```

Comma delimited format is shown in Table 8-7.

**TABLE 8-7**

```
Candidate,Contribution,Donor
"DOLE, ROBERT J",1000,"ANDERSON, WILLIAM J"
"DOLE, ROBERT J",1000,"BARNES, WALLACE"
"DOLE, ROBERT J",1000,"BARRE, HELEN"
"DOLE, ROBERT J",1000,"BARRETT, GABRIELLE"
"DOLE, ROBERT J",1000,"BARRETT, ROBERT E"
"DOLE, ROBERT J",1000,"BEATIE, RUSSEL H"
"DOLE, ROBERT J",1000,"BECKWITH, GILBERT"
"DOLE, ROBERT J",1000,"BEZAMAL, ADOLFO"
"DOLE, ROBERT J",1000,"BIBLE, GEOFFREY C"
```

*Comma delimited* format is used to save space. Instead of having blank spaces between columns, the columns are shoved together. Computer programs know to end a column when they see a comma. The quotation marks tell the software that the words in between should go into character fields. The other information is numeric. (In addition, you often can put field names in the first row to save yourself the time of typing them in again and again.)

*Fixed format* files are a little tricky because sometimes it is necessary to set up a file to catch the information in the proper column. This involves several steps:

1. Build a database (just like you did in Chapter 4) according to the record layout you received.

2. Compare your database and the record layout to the raw information.

3. Instead of entering data, pour the data from another file into the proper columns in your file.

Once you have imported information a few times, you'll get the hang of it pretty quickly. The next chapter will discuss some of the tricks of importing.

## ■≡≡ CHAPTER SUMMARY

❐ You can locate databases by looking for computers on your beat or asking where printouts come from.

❐ Federal and state agencies are putting more and more of their database listings online.

❐ In their reports, consultants and auditors identify databases that you might not know about otherwise.

❐ Always get proper documentation for a database, and always try to get the database for free.

❐ Know the laws relating to electronic access.

❐ Most database manager and spreadsheet software can import most files.

## ▣≣ SUGGESTED TASKS

☐ Go to a local agency that has a public database and request the database.

☐ Copy the database onto your computer.

☐ Open or import the database in Microsoft Excel or Microsoft Access.

☐ Do two relevant calculations and two relevant groupings.

# Dirty Data: Pitfalls and Solutions

Many journalists have used a database that gives details of federal contracts, such as which agency awarded the contract, which company received it, the amount, the year, and the place where work on the contract will be carried out. Lurking in the database is a column of information called "type of obligation." The column (or field) contains one character of information—either "A" or "B"—right after the "dollars" field. Part of the actual layout is shown in Table 9-1.

| TABLE 9-1 | | | |
|---|---|---|---|
| Data Element | Type Data | No. Chars. | Position |
| Kind of Contract Action | A | 1 | 334 |
| Dollars (in thousands) | N | 8 | 315-322 |
| Type of Obligation | A | 1 | 323 |

If you don't pay attention to the "type of obligation" field, you can end up with completely erroneous data.

Why? Because all the dollar amounts posted in the contract database are positive. If obligation type is "A," the dollar amount remains positive. If obligation type is "B," however, it indicates the contract was withdrawn, and thus the dollar amount should

**170**

be read as negative. If obligation type is "B," you must multiply the dollar amount by –1.

There is no problem if you know to ask what "obligation type" means or if the agency that distributes the data tells you its meaning, but this is not always the case. In fact, several journalists have narrowly dodged a budgetary bullet only because they thought to recheck the database, compare it with paper summary reports, and check back with the agency. If they had neglected to multiply certain dollar amounts by –1, they would have been off by hundreds of millions of dollars when they added up the dollar column.

The lesson is this: you must never implicitly trust the data. No database is perfect. No database is complete. Every database is likely to contain a misleading or tricky column. Indeed, George Landau, formerly the computer guru at the *St. Louis Post-Dispatch*, says that all databases are bad databases. You just have to find out how bad.

Good journalists know that they shouldn't trust what anyone tells them until they check the information. (The cliché is: if your mother tells you she loves you, check it out.) That same skepticism must be applied to databases.

Penny Loeb, a senior editor at *U.S. News & World Report* who has done computer-assisted reporting for many years, has said, "I always spot-check. I'm always thinking what could go wrong."[1]

## ▬▬ Record Layout

Before we delve into misleading databases and data, we need to review a record layout. From the previous chapter, you know that you need a record layout if you are going to acquire a database. As mentioned, the record layout acts as a road map for the database. It tells you the name of the field of information; whether the field contains letters and numbers, just numbers, or dates; and the width of the column, which indicates how many letters or numbers can fit in the particular column.

---

[1] Harnessing Computers to Cover News. *The Forum* (September 1993), p. 6.

Remember also that you need the code sheet or codebook that goes with the database. Without the codes, you cannot know that "1" means white or that "4" means felony.

You also know you may have to argue and plead to obtain a database, possibly spending months persuading a bureaucrat to release it to you. And you know that once you have it, you will be pleased you won the battle. Unfortunately, you may find that obtaining the database is only the beginning of the struggle.

## ▮▰▰▰ RECORD LAYOUT MISCUES

Many journalists doing computer-assisted reporting have discovered errors in the record layout, the codebook, and the information itself. Moreover, "the record layout—while important—doesn't tell you everything you need to know about a database," says Shawn McIntosh, now managing editor of the *Jackson Clarion Ledger*.[2] She points out that although a field may be in the layout, it does not necessarily mean there is any information in it.

For example, FBI crime statistics for several states do not list rapes because of a disagreement over the definition of rape. Moreover, state bail databases often lack the critical information about whether a defendant could post bond and get out of jail. Sometimes, the agency has removed, or redacted, the information without saying so.

Let's discuss some of the possible problems in record layouts.

The sample layout in Table 9-2 shows how the information might appear within the columns.

| TABLE 9-2 | | |
|---|---|---|
| **Field** | **Type** | **Length** |
| First name | Character | 15 |
| Last name | Character | 20 |
| Agency | Character | 20 |
| Salary | Numeric | 6 |

---

[2] McIntosh, S. CAJ's Dirty Secrets. *Quill* (September 1993), p. 23.

In this example, you look at the information before importing it into your database manager. You see the first two records, which are shown in Table 9-3.

| TABLE 9-3 | | | | |
|---|---|---|---|---|
| Paul | Jones | Social Services | 15541 | 10/12/1991 |
| Dawn | Brown | Comptroller | 21203 | 05/06/1989 |

Already you notice that something looks wrong. According to Table 9-2, there should be only four columns of information. But in Table 9-3, there is an extra column that looks like a date. What probably happened is that when the database was first put together, the designer decided not to include the date of hire. Later, the designer thought it should be included.

When you are ready to import information into your database manager, you usually have to set up the structure to hold the information. The database structure generally is a mirror of the record layout. In this example, the database structure you set up (shown in Table 9-4) would look a lot like the record layout given in Table 9-2.

| TABLE 9-4 | | |
|---|---|---|
| *Field* | *Type* | *Length* |
| Firstname | Text | 15 |
| Lastname | Text | 20 |
| Agency | Text | 20 |
| Salary | Numeric | 6 |

But if you imported the information shown in Table 9-3 into that layout, it would fall into the wrong fields. The first few records might look like those shown in Table 9-5 (p. 174). As you see in Table 9-5, the information has shifted and is falling into the wrong fields.

| TABLE 9-5 | | | |
|-----------|----------|-----------------|-------------|
| *Firstname* | *Lastname* | *Agency* | *Salary* |
| Paul | Jones | Social Services | 15541 |
| 10/12/1991 | Dawn | Brown | Comptroller |

A real-life instance of the problem of shifting information happened not to a journalist but to the federal court system in Connecticut. In Hartford, the court system made use of a voter list to send out notices for jury duty. To get people's names, the court imported a voter registration list into a database it created. Well, Hartford has a large minority population, whereas towns outside Hartford are largely white. Lawyers soon started to notice that the prospective jurors were mostly white. Eventually, an investigation found that data processors for the court had misread the record layout for voter registration. Instead of allowing eight spaces for the town's name, Hartford, they allowed only seven spaces. Thus, "Hartford" became "Hartfor." The truncation would not have been a problem, except that the following field gave the person's life status. In that field, "d" stood for "dead." Of course, the court didn't want to send jury summonses to dead people, so it created a program that excluded anyone with a status of "d" from its mailing list. And, to the court's computer, everyone in Hartford was dead.

Clearly, it is important to check the record layout against the actual data. It is not uncommon to be given an old record layout or an incomplete one.

## ▉▬ HEADER-ACHES

You finally persuade an agency to give you information in an electronic form rather than on a printout. You get the record layout and disk, rush back to your office, and transfer the information onto your computer's hard drive. You then browse through the information and what do you see? A horror show of headers.

Headers are the bits of information, such as date and page number, that go across the top of a printout page. They have no place in the database of columns and rows. An example of misplaced headers is given in Table 9-6.

| TABLE 9-6 | | | |
|---|---|---|---|
| **Date 02/02/93    Administrative Services    Page 3** | | | |
| **Name** | **Town** | **Zip** | **Salary** |
| Gerald Sun | Lincoln | 06230 | 20,423 |
| Mary Moon | Jefferson | 93914 | 34,433 |

The agency—through incompetence, laziness, or nastiness— apparently provided the image of each printed-out page instead of the raw data. Fortunately, the problem can be corrected with a word processor or database manager or special software. (We won't go through every step, but we'll go over the basic idea of what you can do.)

If you can import the information into a database, you will likely end up with nonsense records at the beginning of each row that starts with "date." For example, the information might look like that shown in Table 9-7.

| TABLE 9-7 | | | |
|---|---|---|---|
| **Name** | **Town** | **Zip** | **Salary** |
| **Date 02/02/93    Administrative Services    Page 3** | | | |
| Gerald Sun | Lincoln | 06230 | 20,423 |
| Mary Moon | Jefferson | 93914 | 34,433 |

But with a "where" statement—such as "delete all records where name like 'Date%'"—you can locate the offending records and eliminate them. (The "%" is a wildcard, standing for any letter or number that follows "Date," such as "Dates" or "Date234." It is used in conjunction with "like" in Fox Pro.) With a word processing program or specialized programs, you can eliminate the headers before importing the information into a database.

## ▆▆▆▆ MEANINGLESS CODES

Probably more common than a bad record layout is an incomplete or inaccurate code sheet. As mentioned previously, the codes must be translated or you'll be lost in a forest of numbers. So you need to make sure the codes are accurate.

Let's say a code sheet defines ethnicity by numbers: "1" for white, "2" for black, "3" for Hispanic, and "4" for other. Once you have imported the information into your database, you perform a standard integrity check. You run a query that asks for the number of records for each race. The result is shown in Table 9-8.

| TABLE 9-8 | |
| --- | --- |
| *Ethnicity* | *Totals* |
| 1 | 550 |
| 2 | 430 |
| 3 | 255 |
| 4 | 77 |
| 7 | 2 |
| 8 | 1 |
| 9 | 113 |

What's going on? Why are there so few totals for ethnic groups 7 and 8? Well, the "7" or "8" could be data-entry errors. No one can type hundreds or thousands of numbers without getting a few wrong. You call the agency and verify that groups 7 and 8 are errors. But group 9 cannot be ignored. You phone the agency again and learn that they used "9" when ethnicity wasn't indicated. But they forgot to put that on their code sheet.

In another example, you might be given all the expenditures for every agency in a state. The agencies are listed not by name but by identification numbers, which range from 1001 through

4999. You run a query in which you group the identification numbers and sum the amount column. Table 9-9 shows what the top of the result might look like.

| TABLE 9-9 | |
| --- | --- |
| *Agency* | *Total (in thousands)* |
| 1022 | $255,321 |
| 4077 | $121,444 |
| 5019 | $ 23,655 |

The result includes an agency identification number, 5019, that does not exist on the code sheet. This happens quite frequently. For example, many states add and eliminate agencies after the election of a new governor. Often, new identification numbers are added to the database but not to the code sheet.

## ■▬▬ SORRY, WRONG NUMBER

The opening of this chapter indicated that it's easy to make mistakes in the millions. You must check to see that all the numbers add up, or at least come close.

In the previous chapter, you learned (1) to ask how many records you would receive in a database, and (2) to ask for hard-copy reports. You also need to do an outer integrity check. In fact, journalists performed an outer check to find out about obligation type in the example about the federal contracts database. In that case, the outer check involved finding a hard-copy report that totaled the dollar amounts of federal contracts for each state and comparing it to the totals from the database.

For federal contracts, you would group the agencies and sum the dollars. Then you would compare the sum for each agency with a hard-copy report.

An outer integrity check not only protects against errors but can lead to excellent news stories. Elliot Jaspin performed a simple integrity check when he received a computer tape of low-interest mortgages given out by a Rhode Island agency to low- and moderate-income residents. Working at the *Providence*

*Journal Bulletin* at the time, Jaspin totaled the amount of mortgages in the database and compared his figure to the totals published in an annual report. The difference was millions of dollars.

But Jaspin had not made a mistake. Apparently, the agency had been hiding a slush fund out of which it made loans to the unqualified friends and relatives of politicians. A phone call from Jaspin about the discrepancy worried the agency, which began shredding documents. Soon thereafter, the state police raided the agency, investigations ensued, and numerous indictments were handed down.

Dollar amounts are not the only thing that can go awry. One quick outer integrity check can involve counting the number of records in your database and comparing it with the number the agency said it gave you. If the numbers don't match, you have a serious problem.

However, the situation can be worse. When it is worse, you need to think of all the integrity checks you can do. I once asked for attendance records for 10,000 state employees. The records showed how the employees spent every working hour—whether it was regular time, overtime, sick time, vacation, or personal days. The agency that gave me the records said it had forgotten to do a record count; but because it gave me 1.8 million attendance records, which is what I had counted, I thought I had them all.

However, after a while it occurred to me that I probably should have records for at least 250 days for each employee. Even if an employee left part way through the year, another employee would be earning overtime in his or her place. A quick calculation of 10,000 employees times 250 days results in 2.5 million records. It took two days of arguing, but the agency finally looked at its own work, found a serious programming error, and acknowledged that it had shortchanged me by 700,000 records.

## ■▬▬▬ MAINFRAME MISERY IN NUMBERS AND LETTERS

Although some journalists have success with mainframe computers, most are doing computer-assisted reporting work on IBM-compatible PCs or Macintosh computers. Yet mainframes haunt most personal computer–based journalists. Not only do

mainframes supply a wealth of gibberish languages and practices, they also supply bad advice in layouts and bothersome letters. Several common examples follow.

A layout from a mainframe operation often specifies a
numeric type of field for zip codes and identification numbers.
But when you import this information into a database manager on a PC, you may face enormous problems. For example,
if you tell some database managers to import the zip code
or identification number into the numeric field, it will cause
significant damage. If the database manager sees a zip code
that begins with a "0," it will eliminate the "0" at the beginning
of the zip code because it looks meaningless.

Thus, for journalists who work with zip codes that begin
with "0" (such as 01776), all zip codes will be rendered in a database manager as four characters (1776) instead of five. Those
zip codes will be useless, not only for mailing addresses, but
also for matching one database to another.

The same problem can happen with identification codes. An
employee with the identification number 042325 in a mainframe
will have it rendered as 42325 in a database manager. This will
also prevent accurate matches.

The way to escape this peril is to always import zip codes,
identification numbers, and phone numbers into character
fields. Generally, import as a character field any number that
will never be added, subtracted, multiplied, or divided. The
database manager then will preserve all the digits.

Fields that contain dates can be another bugaboo. Many
journalists split the field into three fields (day, month, year)
to make things simpler. Others import the dates into character
fields. Cleaning up dates is a problem even for the more advanced.

Another mainframe misery that haunts journalists is the
wonderful world of the programming language COBOL. If an
agency uses COBOL, it is quite possible that after importing you
will get a funny-looking number where you expect to see a dollar amount. Instead of 45222 (as in $452.22), you might get
4522B. In the case of 4522B, you need to somehow add the digit
"2" to the number. Moreover, you will have to fix other numbers
as well. If there is an "A," it means "1." The letter "F" stands for
"6," and so on. Altogether, there are 10 letters, each standing for
"0" through "9."

Dealing with this problem involves two strategies we have already encountered.

First, when you import the numbers, make the "Hartfor" mistake intentionally. With 4522B, you would create two fields instead of one by truncating the "amount" field. One field—call it "amount"—would contain all numbers up to the letter (in this example, 4522); the second field ("letter") would contain only the "B."

Then, you would create another field called "newamount" and write a "replace" statement. The replace statement is tricky because you are appending a digit, *not* adding it to the number.

You want the number to look like 45222. You need to put an extra digit in the number, so you multiply it by 10 and add 2. Your command would read:

Replace all newamount with (amount*10) +
2 for letter = "B"

The "amount*10" turns 4522 into 45220. Now you can safely add the 2 to get 45222.

Then, if you want to convert the number to dollars and cents, you would write:

Replace all newamount with newamount*.01

Now you have 452.22.

This may seem like a lot of time-consuming work, but it's good to know. Not only might you face this problem, but the exercise shows you how to think about data and how to clean data. The idea of separating a field into two or more parts is crucial when you get into more complex data cleaning.

## OFFENSIVE CHARACTERS

Databases can contain offensive characters. They may be weird-looking smiling faces or misplaced commas or semicolons. Before importing information into a database, you should get rid of such characters. Most word processing programs allow you to do this fairly easily.

One old program, Xywrite, allows you to write a "search and destroy" instruction. Let's say you want to eliminate commas in the data. You would write "CH/,//" at the top of the computer screen. "CH" means change. The slash marks ("/,/") tell the program that you want to eliminate whatever is between—in this case, the comma. In the next gap between slash marks, you would leave no space. (You could also replace the comma with another symbol by typing that symbol, or put in a space by typing a space. Do not include quotation marks.) When you hit the "Enter" key, the software will go through your database and eliminate every comma it finds.

There is a fancier way to do this with database programs, using tools called *string functions*. String functions are a powerful, but sometimes confusing, way to clean data. A *string* is a series of letters or numbers or other symbols, such as commas in a field. A string function is a command that allows you to alter data in a field.

For example, a string function can permit you to split a field based on a comma or space in the middle of a field. This can be handy when you are trying to match names in one table with names in another. One table may put the first name in a separate field and the last name in another field. But another table may put the last and first name in the same field, such as "Smith, John." To make the names in the second field useful for a match, you can use the comma as a marker to split the name into a first name field and a last name field.

## PARSING

Parsing has long been a popular way of doing data cleaning in spreadsheets. Parsing means drawing column lines between different kinds of data. One drawback is that spreadsheets can only handle up to 64,000 records. Another is that parsing is somewhat awkward.

A new spreadsheet feature will look at a text file when you open it and suggest column lines. If the text file is in tabular format (i.e., it is arranged in columns), the spreadsheet can rapidly arrange the data. This is especially handy for small files downloaded from online sources. Remember the campaign finance data in Chapter 4? Table 9-10 is what it would look like if you downloaded it as tabular data. The spreadsheet enables you to do that easily. As shown in Table 9-10, you can draw lines between the text columns by clicking. You can delete them by putting the cursor on the line and double-clicking.

**TABLE 9-10**

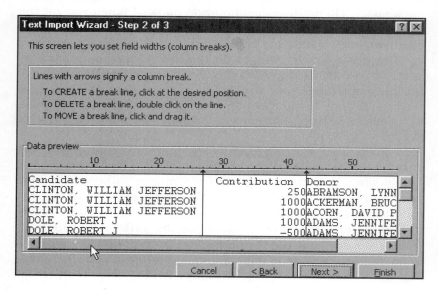

## ■▬ TWO RULES

There are two cardinal rules for dealing with dirty data.

First, never work on the original database. Instead, create a copy of the database, and do your work there. Then, if you make a mistake, you will be able to recover and start again. You can't do that if you have changed the original file. Also, as you work with the data, save each major change to the data as a different file, with sequential numbering. This creates an audit trail of your work. For example, working with census data, your first census file might be "states1." The first copy would be "states2," and the next copy "states3."

Second, if you need to standardize spellings, never do it in the original field. Always create a new field. That way, you don't change the original and thus you can compare the field you have cleaned to the original information and ensure you did not incorrectly change the data.

## ■▬▬ Dirty Data

Once you start doing computer-assisted reporting, it won't be long before you say, "How dirty is the data?" Dirty data usually begins with sloppy typing. Remember that the information in a database has been entered by someone who was doing one of the most boring jobs in the world. Agencies and businesses pay low wages to data-entry clerks, which doesn't help morale. Often, an agency is too understaffed to do proper integrity checks; and even if it does do them, errors often slip through.

Whenever you obtain a new database, browse through the top 100 records to look for misspellings and nonsense. You also should run queries that use the *distinct* function. If the database contains town names, run a query that asks how many distinct spellings there are. (Often, the same town can be spelled in several different ways.) If the database (e.g., about truck accidents) contains designations for interstate highways, "Interstate 70" might appear as "I-70," "I 70," and "Interstate 70." Other federal or state records might spell "St. Louis" as "Saint Louis," "St. Louis," and "St Louis."

Unless you clean the data or do manual calculations, such variations will hurt your ability to do accurate analysis. Remember, to a computer, a space and a hyphen make the information look different. To a database manager, "St. Louis" and "St Louis" are different towns.

Sometimes, you can get the work done by referring only to a string of letters in a "where" statement. Perhaps the statement "where highway = 70" will be good enough, or "where town = Louis." But unless you know the database well, that kind of "where" statement can be dangerous. For example, let's say you have a database of gun dealers, and you want to count the number in St. Louis. If you run a query to count them, you will get a display like that shown in Table 9-11 (p. 184).

| TABLE 9-11 | |
|---|---|
| St Louis | 22 |
| St. Louis | 24 |
| Saint Louis | 4 |

With a pencil or calculator, you could add the figures in the table to determine that there are 50 gun dealers in St. Louis. But if you have a lot of records, you wouldn't want to do that. You could use a "where" statement that looks at the string of letters, but a better approach involves adding a field called "newname."

Once you have a new field, you can write a "where" statement that defines all possible spellings of a name and tells the database manager to change the names to one spelling and put the changes in "newname." In the FoxPro software, the language would be as follows:

Replace all newname with "St. Louis" for name =
"St Louis" or name = "St. Louis" or name = "Saint Louis"

("Replace all" means to replace every "newname" field.)

You also can use an update command, which might be easier and more efficient in certain softwares. In this case, if the table name was *highway*, you would write:

Update highway
Set newname = "St. Louis"
where name   = "St Louis" or name = "St. Louis" or
name = "Saint Louis"

In either case, your result is shown in Table 9-12:

| TABLE 9-12 | |
|---|---|
| *Town* | *Newname* |
| St Louis | St. Louis |
| St. Louis | St. Louis |
| Saint Louis | St. Louis |

Now, if you wanted to count all the gun dealers in St. Louis, you could write a query that used "newname" and counted the number of gun dealers. The result is shown in Table 9-13.

| TABLE 9-13 | |
| --- | --- |
| St. Louis | 50 |

Remember, no database is perfect or complete; but that doesn't mean it cannot be made usable.

## ■≡ CHAPTER SUMMARY

❏ Know how many records are supposed to be in the database.

❏ Watch for missing words in a database.

❏ Make sure that identification and zip codes in a database contain all numbers.

❏ Match the record layout carefully to the actual data in a database.

❏ Use word processors or string functions to correct errors in database managers.

❏ Use spreadsheet parsing when the number of records is small.

❏ Compare total amounts in a database to hard-copy reports.

## ■≡ SUGGESTED TASKS

❏ Get part of the Federal Election Commission contributor database.

❏ Using a database manager, create a new field called "occupation2."

❏ Use the "Update" and/or "Replace" functions to turn the occupation field into something more useful in the "occupation2" field.

*Hint:* Copy all the occupations into the new field before beginning your work. It's easier to correct a record than to type it in.

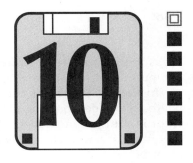

# GETTING GOING:
# STRATEGIES FOR STORIES

You have the computer and the software and the realization that the judicious and skillful use of these tools can create good news stories. Now what? If you're not careful, you can suffer a severe case of reporter's block trying to figure out what stories to do. Worse, a large database will swallow you up with its complexities, and it will take you years to finish the story.

You can avoid these perils with a few key strategies.

## START SMALL

Ralph Frammolino, a *Los Angeles Times* reporter, spent a few hours typing into a database manager the details about 90 or so prospective jurors for the O. J. Simpson murder trial. A quick review of the data found trends that resulted in two stories in two days, one on jurors' beliefs about DNA testing that appeared on the front page.

When working as a reporter in New Jersey, Neil Reisner, a former NICAR trainer now at the *Miami Herald*, typed into a spreadsheet the voter registration numbers for towns in five counties. He then wrote a story for the Sunday paper that showed how lack of registration by Democrats played a critical role in the outcome of a gubernatorial election.

Many other reporters, such as Carol Napolitano of the *Omaha World Herald* and Heather Newman of the *Detroit Free*

*Press,* constantly turn around quick articles by supple use of computer-assisted reporting for stories on the beat.

In the 1980s, it was almost a matter of pride for a journalist to use a database composed of hundreds of thousands of records. But for journalists in the 1990s, some of the most effective stories came from only a few hundred or a few thousand records.

Starting with a small database allows you to get to know the information. Look for databases that involve only a few columns of names or numbers. If you really have to or want to, you can manually check the database—and doing so will improve your confidence in the information and in your skills.

Journalists today have an advantage over journalists in the 1980s. In the 1980s, most databases came from mainframe computer tapes. They had to be downloaded and broken up into smaller parts to be used on personal computers. Nowadays, however, many databases are already reduced in size at online sites or on disks. For example, some large databases, such as census files, are already broken into small databases. Journalists have used small census files for stories on housing, income, transportation, and ethnic diversity in cities.

## ▪▬▬▬ BUILD YOUR OWN DATABASE

As we saw in Frammolino's and Reisner's stories, reporters shouldn't be afraid of building their own databases. If you build your own database, you immediately take three steps toward a successful story. One, you become very familiar with the information because of the attention to detail you have to give it. Two, because data entry is so tedious, you will keep the information small and to the point. Three, if you had to build a database, then no one else has it—and you probably have an exclusive story.

Corky Johnson, a TV reporter, has built several databases for solid stories, including pieces on the sale of salvaged cars and absenteeism at a county office.

At the *Hartford Courant,* environmental writer Daniel Jones, researcher Leah Segal, and I built an abbreviated database on emissions of toxic chemicals by manufacturers, after we learned that we would have to wait nine months for governmental officials to release their database. By doing so, we learned a lot about how companies filled out the hard-copy reports, and we learned that, because of administrative decisions, the state had not mentioned 20 percent of the emissions in its reports. No one else had the information for months, and we used the database for several exclusive stories.

## ■▬▬ MATCH THE DATABASE TO YOUR KNOWLEDGE

Although electronic databases permit you to learn about and explore new subjects, it's better to start with a database on something you know about. Building your own database is one way to be sure of the information and how to use it; getting a database on a topic you know about and cover is another way.

A database is a mirror of reality, and a mirror always has flaws. You need to know how flawed the mirror is and how distorted the image. That's why it's good to get a database about your own beat or specialty. The database can highlight problems or provide tips about the subject, but it also can present only a small portion of it.

If you aren't working on a story about a subject with which you are familiar, then team up with a reporter who knows it. When I worked on a judicial story, I worked with the court reporter. On other subjects, I worked with the environmental reporter, the medical reporter, the city hall reporters, or the political reporters. They pointed out problems in the databases, while using the patterns and clues the databases revealed.

## ■▬▬ THE MINIMUM STORY

When you are starting out, never get a database without thinking what the minimum story is. By "minimum story," we mean the surest, most basic story available.

If you get a database of governmental salaries, you can be pretty sure that you will have a story about the average, the median, and who gets the highest and lowest. If you get a database of housing prices over the past few years, you can be confident that you will have a story about changes and trends. If you get a database on crime, you will undoubtedly be able to report on increases and decreases. If you get a database on political contributions, you will have a story about who gave the least and the most and where the contributors were from.

These are minimum stories. They don't always become the lead story of the day, but they are solid and enable you to do good public service journalism. They also provide you with a foundation of databases that bolster later stories or that can be combined with new databases for even better stories.

## KEEP UP WITH OTHER REPORTERS' WORK

Whether it's traditional reporting or computer-assisted reporting, too many journalists get caught up in the argument that a story has been done before. Frankly, most stories have been done before. That's not the point. The real questions are whether your story is a good one, whether the previous stories have been done thoroughly and correctly, and whether your material is worthwhile.

The same applies to databases. After all, a reporter in one community can do a reasonably good overview of who deals guns in that community. Possibly there is no shattering news, just an interesting look at the issue. But you may get the same database for your own community and find that many gun dealers are police officers, and that some of them sell guns to convicted felons. It's the quality of the database and what you do with it that counts.

Therefore, try to keep up with what other journalists are doing. When you read or hear about a journalist who has used a database or an online resource that you may be interested in, review the stories to determine how the source might be applicable in your own situation. You also can call (or email) the journalist for tips on the database.

The National Institute for Computer-Assisted Reporting (NICAR) offers books that contain brief descriptions of how two computer-assisted stories were done by print and broadcast journalists, and what databases and software were used. NICAR's listserv and Web site and monthly newsletter, *Uplink,* also give how-to information on computer-assisted reporting.

## ▆▆▆ Integrate Databases into Your Daily Work

Although some journalists use databases only for long projects, you should try to integrate their use into stories on the beat and on the deadline. Indeed, Pat Stith, a veteran investigative journalist at the *Raleigh News & Observer* and a leader there in computer-assisted reporting, gave a good tip when he said, "We are going to use databases to create or improve everyday front page stories and second fronts."

The "improve" part of that statement is especially useful for a journalist beginning to explore computer-assisted reporting. Quietly improve your stories by adding online searches, small spreadsheet calculations, and summary data from database managers. You will be able to increase your expertise without unduly increasing expectations within the news organization.

## ▆▆▆ Find a Partner

If at all possible, find a partner to learn with. Considering the new way of thinking and looking at information, it helps to have someone with whom to talk and discuss solutions to problems. The "buddy system" helps keep you focused and also helps prevent errors. Having a friendly colleague look over your shoulder when you are doing your first queries or calculations will save you a lot of time and trouble. You will also learn faster by helping someone else. With a buddy system, stories are usually more thorough and accurate.

## ▆▆▆ Become Familiar with the Computer Field

Because you are learning a new subject, take the time to read some magazines about computer hardware and software.

Reviews of hardware and software may be difficult to understand, but they can help you learn the language and find tools that might help you do a better job.

You should also get to know people who work in the computer field but who are not journalists themselves. They often have a quick answer for a problem that has baffled you.

## ◼️▤ Look for Tips

Keep a narrow focus when you start doing CAR stories, but don't overlook potentially good stories or tips in databases. When you have finished your minimum story, set aside a half hour to peruse a database. Look for tips by searching for particular words, by looking for "outliers," by creating summary data, by doing percentages, or by just scanning the databases. Often, a good story can emerge from such a scan.

## ◼️▤ Get Excited

The lasting attraction of computer-assisted reporting is that it allows you to do stories you never could have done before, in ways you never thought of. Moreover, you can be creative and responsible at the same time.

Too often, good journalists are stymied by fear, tradition, or cynicism within their own news organizations or universities. Excitement is often regarded with suspicion. But computer-assisted reporting can revive a stodgy, plodding organization with new, in-depth looks at a community. Don't miss the chance to enjoy it.

## ◼️▤ Chapter Summary

- ❐ Start with small databases.
- ❐ Build your own database.
- ❐ Get databases for subjects you know.

❑ Integrate computer-assisted reporting into your daily work.

❑ Use the buddy system.

❑ Use databases as tipsters.

## ■≡ SUGGESTED TASKS

❑ Examine how other computer-assisted reporting stories were done. (*Hint:* Contact NICAR.)

❑ Obtain a database on city or county employee salaries, including name, title, department, salary, and date of hire.

❑ Import the database into Microsoft Access or another database manager.

❑ Determine which 10 employees receive the most pay annually.

❑ Determine which 10 employees receive the least pay annually.

❑ Determine which department pays the highest average salary.

❑ Determine if employees who have worked there 10 years or more make, on average, more than those who have worked there less than 10 years.

❑ Transfer the database, or part of it, into a spreadsheet program such as Microsoft Excel.

❑ Determine which department pays the highest median salary.

❑ Compare that figure to the highest average salary.

❑ Interview officials about your findings and verify your numbers are correct.

❑ Write a story about your findings.

❑ Build a database for your Rolodex.

❑ Enter the data from your Rolodex into the database.

# APPENDIX A

## CHOOSING EQUIPMENT AND SOFTWARE

Equipment and software change monthly, if not weekly. Therefore, you need to answer the following questions in order:

❏ What kind of databases do I intend to research or analyze?

❏ What software do I need to perform these analyses?

❏ What kind of hardware do I need to run the software, and how much space on the computer do I need?

If you plan to crunch numbers, analyze large databases, and go online, then you can quickly identify the software you need. At a minimum, you will need a database manager, a spreadsheet, and online software. The storage and memory requirements of the software will guide you in your selection of hardware. If you are going to do statistics or mapping, you will need as much space and memory as you can get.

Also, find out what kind of software your colleagues are using. You may want to choose the same software, because they are familiar with it and can help you learn it.

For most database manager software now on the market, you will need at least 1 gigabyte to 2 gigabytes on your hard drive and 64 megabytes of RAM. Get more than 64 megabytes if at all possible.

Your computer, if IBM-compatible, should have the highest Pentium processor you can afford. (The higher the megahertz, the faster it goes.) If you are using a Macintosh, choose a processor with the highest-speed Power PC chip. Your modem should have a speed of at least 33.6 bps in order to handle Web graphics. If you can afford it, a modem with a higher speed is better.

Because of the graphics in software, a color monitor—preferably a 17-inch one—is a must on a laptop or desktop computer.

For software, journalists frequently use the following spread-sheets: Microsoft Excel, Quattro Pro for Windows, and Lotus 1-2-3. They frequently use the following database managers: Microsoft Access, Microsoft FoxPro, or Paradox for Windows.

For Internet access, almost every day a new provider appears with a new kind of software. Netscape Communications Corp.'s software and Microsoft Explorer are the ones most often used.

Journalists also are using statistical software. The two most popular are SPSS, produced by SPSS Inc. in Chicago, and SAS, produced by the SAS Institute in Cary, N.C. Many journalists favor SPSS because, as with many other software packages, you pay only once to buy a license. SAS, on the other hand, charges an annual license fee.

Journalists nowadays often use mapping software. As discussed in Chapter 5, mapping software allows you to take street addresses or other geographical database information and put it onto a map. The most popular software package is ArcView (produced by ESRI, found at <www.esri.com>) and MapInfo (produced by MapInfo Corp. in Troy, N.Y., at <www.mapinfo.com-homepage .html>).

To keep up with hardware and software changes, prices, and quality, read commercial computer magazines.

# APPENDIX **B**

## PLACES TO START ONLINE

Online resources are changing daily, but here are a few "starter sites" that journalists have found easy to use and helpful. This list is by no means complete, and everyone has his or her favorites. Remember that it is not uncommon for addresses to change.

The last three letters of a Web site's address give a clue about who has put it together. There are seven major categories, but expect them to increase.

| | |
|---|---|
| *.com* | commercial |
| *.edu* | education |
| *.gov* | government |
| *.int* | international |
| *.mil* | military |
| *.net* | networking organization |
| *.org* | nonprofit organization |

## ■▬ WORLD WIDE WEB SITES

### Web Site Searchers (Guides and Search Tools)

Search tools allow to you to search other Web sites for information you need. (You can find more search tools on the homepages of Web browsers such as Netscape.)

❑  http://www.altavista.digital.com
❑  http://www.excite.com
❑  http://www.hotbot.com
❑  http://www.lycos.com
❑  http://www.yahoo.com

## People and Business Finders

The following sites allow you to search for phone numbers, addresses, and email addresses. Some also supply a map showing how to get to the addresses.

❏ http://www.switchboard.com

❏ http://www.databaseamerica.com

❏ http://www.bigfoot.com

❏ http://www.whowhere.com

❏ http://www.four11.com

## Government Site Finders

Fedworld.gov is a gateway to many other federal agencies. Campaignfinance.org has an index of links to all state Web sites.

❏ http://www.fedworld.gov

❏ http://www.campaignfinance.org

❏ http://www.globalcomputing.com.states.html

## Government and Informational Sites

❏ *The U.S. Census Bureau*   For census information and links to other statistical sites:
http://www.census.gov

❏ *U.S. General Accounting Office*   For audits, investigations, and reports done by the audit team of Congress:
http://www.gao.gov

❏ *Library of Congress*   For a wealth of federal information and links to other good sites:
http://www.loc.gov

❏ *Thomas site* (as in Thomas Jefferson)   Legislative indexes and information on congressional bills:
http://thomas.loc.gov

❏ *CIA World Factbook*   Information about demographics and statistics about other countries:
http://www.odci.gov/cia/publications/factbook/index.html

## Private Organizations Helpful to Journalists

❐ *The Reporters Committee for Freedom of the Press*
http://www.rcfp.org

❐ *First Amendment Center at the Freedom Forum*
http://www.freedomforum.org/first/welcome.asp

❐ *ProfNet* ProfNet, a network of public relations people, can lead you to experts.
http://www.profnet.com

❐ *American Journalism Review* *American Journalism Review*'s links to Web sites of newspapers in the United States and around the world.
http://www.newslink.org/news.html

❐ *All-Links* All-Links provides connections to newspapers around the world.
http://www.all-links.com

## ▰▰▰ NEWSGROUP SEARCHES

Newsgroups are discussion groups, but you don't receive mail from them. You visit the newsgroup on a topic in which you are interested and read the postings. One convenient way to check out newsgroups is through two Web sites, <http://www.dejanews.com> and <http://www.altavista.digital.com>, and by changing the search area from the Web to "Usenet."

## ▰▰▰ LISTSERVS

Listservs are discussion groups in which (1) you receive every message sent to the listserv by a member, and (2) every one of your messages is sent to every other member. See Chapter 7 for information on how to subscribe to listservs.

Several listservs and their email addresses are given below:

❐ CARR-L Computer-Assisted Reporting and Research
listserv@ulkyvm.louisville.edu

❏ FOI-L   Freedom of Information
  listserv@listserv.syr.edu
❏ IRE-L   Investigative Reporters and Editors
  listserv@mizzou1.missouri.edu
❏ JOURNET   Journalism Education
  listserv@qucdn.Queensu.Ca
❏ NEWSLIB   News Research
  listserv@gibbs.oit.unc.edu
❏ NICAR-L   National Institute for Computer-Assisted Reporting
  listserv@lists.missouri.edu
❏ SHOPTALK   Broadcast News
  listserv@.syr.edu


## ▒▒▒ FURTHER READING

There are countless books and Web sites dealing with the Internet and online resources.

Here are some good starting points for finding practical resources:

*Computer Assisted Research*, Nora Paul, Poynter Institute, at <http://www.poynter.org/car/cg_chome.htm>.
*How to Access the Federal Government on the Internet 1999*, Bruce Maxwell, Congressional Quarterly Books, 1998.
*How to Access the Government's Electronic Bulletin Boards*, Bruce Maxwell, Congressional Quarterly Books, 1997.
*A Journalist's Guide to the Internet*, Christopher Callahan, Allyn & Bacon, 1998.
*The NICAR Net-Tour* at <www.nicar.org/nettour/>.

# APPENDIX C

## ETHICS AND ACCURACY IN COMPUTER-ASSISTED REPORTING

The ethics of computer-assisted reporting do not vary from the ethics of traditional or investigative journalism. You will run into the same dilemmas you have met while using paper records and talking to people face to face or on the phone. As in investigative or enterprise reporting, however, with computer-assisted reporting your responsibilities increase because you may be going into territory where others have not gone before and you may have numbers and statistics that must be treated carefully.

An electronic medium enables you to copy documents and contact people quickly. Therefore, it's important to think before you act.

Following are 15 commandments for computer-assisted reporting culled from dozens of journalists:

❐ Always be as fair and accurate as possible.

❐ Quickly acknowledge and correct your errors.

❐ Just because it's electronic or on a computer screen doesn't mean it's right.

❐ Recheck and recheck your numbers. Compare them to last year's. Compare them to hard-copy summary reports. Trust your gut. If the numbers don't "feel" right, check them out until they do.

❐ Check and recheck the graphics and charts that appear with a story. It's your responsibility to make sure they match the story.

❐ Watch out for miscoding and data-entry errors. Just because the government got it wrong doesn't mean you should too.

❐ Don't bend the numbers or results to prove your story. Once your story is done, become a devil's advocate and try to destroy your findings. If you don't, be assured the people who dislike your story will.

❏ Know what every category and code in a database mean. No guessing.

❏ Don't try to do more than you know how to do. (Consult a social scientist if you are getting into social science or statistics.)

❏ Don't trust email or other messages on the Internet any more than you would trust what someone wrote you in an anonymous letter. Verify who is writing before you quote.

❏ Don't hack your way into a private electronic area. Be respectful of privacy. If someone offers you confidential information, consult with editors, news directors, and lawyers before deciding whether to accept it.

❏ Don't use anonymous sources unless it is absolutely necessary.

❏ Respect copyright laws when using Internet sources. Think before you copy.

❏ Identify yourself accurately on the Internet. There are very few stories in journalism for which you can justify misrepresentation. These are special cases that must be discussed with editors, news directors, and lawyers. Just because misrepresentation is easy to do doesn't mean you should do it.

❏ Watch what you write in email or other electronic messages. Don't slander, and don't libel.

# APPENDIX D

## REQUESTS FOR ELECTRONIC INFORMATION

### ▦ SAMPLE LETTER OF REQUEST

On the following page, we present a sample letter of request for a database. Because of the ambiguity of laws and regulations, cite a Freedom of Information Act or a Sunshine Law only if the act or law clearly covers electronic information. Also, whenever possible, fax your letter to the agency.

### ▦ DISKS

Disks, computer tapes, and CD-ROMs can be easy or tricky to work with, depending on how an agency makes its copies. Here is a checklist for requesting information:

❐ How large is the information? How many megabytes?

❐ Is the information from a DOS or Windows system, a Macintosh system, a Unix system, or other system?

❐ From what kind of machine will the information be copied? Mainframe, personal computer, or other? Are any conversions of the database being made from one language to another?

❐ What language will the information be in? Text, spreadsheet, database manager, or other? Can they give it to you in ASCII fixed format or ASCII comma delimited?

❐ How many files are on the disk? What are their names? Are they compressed files? What kind of compression did they use?

SAMPLE LETTER OF REQUEST

Date

Name of agency official
Title
Name of agency
Address
City, state, zip

Dear _____:

    I am requesting a copy of your electronic database on _____. Before a copy is made, however, I first want to obtain a copy of the record layout, information on the format in which it is stored, a printout of the first 100 records, and any unusual details about the database. I also would like to know how many records are in the database, and I would like to obtain copies of all annual printed reports on the database.

    After I have reviewed the details about the database, I would like to discuss the most efficient way to copy the database and the medium to which it will be copied. If there are fees or charges involved in copying the database, I would like a breakdown of those charges before the copy is made.

    If any information is considered private and will be excluded from the copy of the database, I want to know the categories of information that will be excluded and under what privacy law or provisions they are being excluded.

    I would appreciate your handling this request as quickly as possible. If I can do anything to speed up the process or if you need more information, please let me know. I look forward to hearing from you.

Sincerely,
(Signature)

Name
Address
City, state, zip
Phone number
Fax number
Email

## ■▤≡ NINE-TRACK TAPES

Obtaining information on nine-track tapes can be extremely tricky. If you can get the agency to simplify the tape for you without charge, do so. Following is a checklist for ordering a nine-track tape:

❐   What is the tape's density? 6,250 bpi, 1,600 bpi, or other?

❐   What is the record length? Is it fixed or variable? Are the records standard or redefined?

❐   What is the blocking factor or block size?

❐   Is the tape labeled or unlabeled?

❐   Is the database in ASCII or EBCDIC?

❐   What kind of machine is producing the tape? IBM, Hewlett-Packard, Digital Equipment Corporation, or other?

❐   How many records are contained on the tape?

❐   Is there more than one file on the tape?

❐   Has the information been compressed or packed?


## ■▤≡ FURTHER READING

*Access to Electronic Records: A Guide to Reporting on State and Local Government in the Computer Age,* The Reporters Committee for Freedom of the Press, Washington, D.C., 1990.

*The New Precision Journalism,* Philip Meyer, Indiana University Press, Bloomington, Ind., 1991.

*Nine-Track Express,* Elliot Jaspin and Daniel Woods, The Reporters' Software Project, Columbia, Mo. (Call NICAR at 573-882-0684 to obtain this manual, which is self-published.)

# APPENDIX E

## GETTING STORY IDEAS FOR COMPUTER-ASSISTED REPORTING

You can get story ideas by going online and monitoring discussions by practicing journalists, attending seminars and conferences given by the National Institute for Computer-Assisted Reporting and other organizations, reading books and newsletters about computer-assisted reporting, and viewing videotapes of stories by broadcasters using computer-assisted reporting. Here are a few suggestions for getting ideas:

❑ Monitor journalist listservs, such as NICAR-L, IRE-L, and CARR-L.

❑ Visit the NICAR Web site at <http://www.nicar.org>, which has databases and training materials.

❑ Read *101 Computer-Assisted Reporting Stories* and *The 100 Computer-Assisted Stories,* published by Investigative Reporters and Editors and NICAR, and Bruce Garrison's *Computer-Assisted Reporting* (1998), published by Lawrence Erlbaum Associates, Hillsdale, N.J. These books describe computer-assisted stories and how they were done.

❑ Borrow broadcast videotapes from the library at Investigative Reporters and Editors, Columbia, Mo. (phone: 573-882-2042).

❑ Subscribe to *Uplink,* the newsletter of NICAR, Columbia, Mo. (phone: 573-882-0684).

# APPENDIX F

## STRUCTURED QUERY LANGUAGE

As journalists become more sophisticated in computer-assisted reporting, they often learn Structured Query Language (SQL). Some journalists find SQL off-putting at first, but it is an efficient and powerful language commonly used to ask questions of databases. SQL has six basic commands. You do not need to use all of them in every query, but you must always use "select" and "from." Also, the commands must be given in order: *select, from, where, group by, having, order by.* Here are the basic definitions of the commands:

❏ SELECT is a way of choosing the columns of information you want. You can also use it to calculate or to create a new column.

❏ FROM chooses which table or tables of information you want to use.

❏ WHERE allows you to filter the records you want to see.

❏ GROUP BY is a way of summarizing information whenever you do math. It must be used carefully in conjunction with "select."

❏ HAVING allows you to limit the number of records in your answer if you have summarized the records. It is used with "group by."

❏ ORDER BY lets you sort your answer from highest to lowest or lowest to highest by a particular column.

Let's say you are looking at contributions to presidential candidates. You want to total the amounts given to each candidate in the 1996 election, limit your look to those candidates who received more than $1 million, and order them by highest to lowest amount given. Your table of information is called "Contributions." Table F-1 shows how you would do the work in Structured Query Language.

**TABLE F-1**

Select candidate, sum (amount)
From contributions
Where year = "1996"
Group by candidate
Having sum (amount) > 1000000
Order by 2 desc

According to Table F-1, "select" is choosing only the candidates' names and is creating a new column called "sum (amount)." "From" is choosing the table "contributions." "Where" is limiting the contributions to the year 1996. "Group by" is telling the program to sum the amount of contributions according to candidate. "Having" limits the answer to those candidates who received more than $1 million. "Order by" sorts the information by column 2, which is the new column created by "sum (amount)."

Table F-2 shows how the answer might look.

**TABLE F-2**

| | |
|---|---|
| Clinton | 15,000,000 |
| Dole | 5,000,000 |

### ▬▬▬ FURTHER READING

Two handy books on beginning SQL are:

*The Practical SQL Handbook: Using Structured Query Language,* Judith S. Bowman, Sandra L. Emerson, and Marcy Darnovsky, Addison-Wesley Company Inc., Reading, Mass., 1996.

*Understanding SQL,* Martin Gruber, Sybex Inc., Alameda, Calif., 1990.

# APPENDIX G

## COMPRESSING AND DECOMPRESSING INFORMATION

As journalists get more databases online and from disks, they run into compressed files. You compress files by running a program that squeezes the data bits together and takes the "air" or empty space out of the information.

A good compression program can sometimes reduce a 3-megabyte file to half a megabyte or less (depending on the data) so that it fits onto a disk that holds only 1.4 megabytes. Compressed data also take less time to send across a network or over a phone line. But you can't use these data unless you decompress them. If you are lucky, a government agency will give you a self-extracting file that automatically unzips (or expands) itself.

Journalists working on IBM-compatible computers often use a relatively inexpensive commercial program called WinZip. If you don't have it, you should get it. Macintosh users use Stuffit.

For purposes of this appendix, we will do a brief run-through using WinZip.

When you get a "zipped" file, go to WinZip, as in Table G-1, and click "Open."

**TABLE G-1**

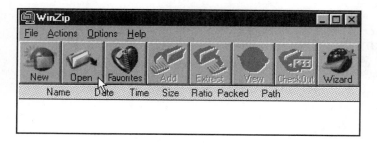

You will get a window called "Open Archive," as in Table G-2. Click on "Open."

**TABLE G-2**

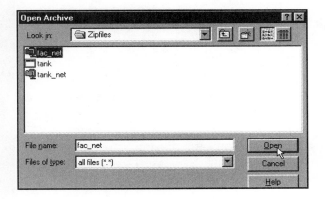

Find and choose the file and click on "Extract" (see Table G-3).

**TABLE G-3**

Then choose the folder to which you want it to be extracted and click to extract, as in Table G-4. (Remember that the zipped file will still exist.)

**TABLE G-4**

To zip a file, click on "New," as in Table G-5.

**TABLE G-5**

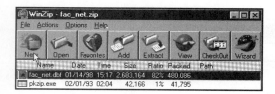

Choose the name of the new file, and click on "OK" (Table G-6).

**TABLE G-6**

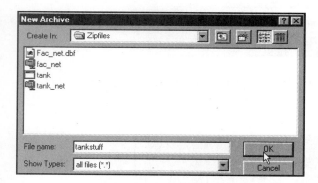

Choose the file or files to zip and the folder to put them in (Table G-7). Click "Add."

**TABLE G-7**

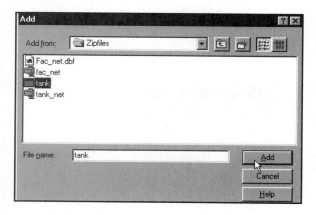

Click on the file name ("tank.exe") to zip it (Table G-8).

**TABLE G-8**

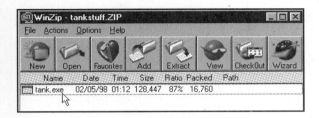

# GLOSSARY

**ASCII (american standard code for information interchange)**
Pronounced ASK-KEY. The way information in 0s and 1s is coded on a personal computer. In a practical sense, an ASCII file looks like a text file and may be used by most word processing programs, spreadsheets, database managers, and other software. When in doubt, ask for a file in ASCII.

**baud** A unit of measure that refers to bandwidth. Often used interchangeably with bits per second (bps), it measures how rapidly information can be transferred online.

**bit** The smallest unit of measuring data. Eight bits make up one byte. A bit can be thought of as a 1 or 0. For example, the letter *A* in ASCII is eight bits in a certain order: 0100 0001.

**Boolean logic** A way of searching online and database information that uses the words *and, or,* and *not.* These words allow a searcher to filter in or filter out categories of information.

**bps (bits per second)** Used to count the number of bits transferred in a second in an online connection. For example, a speed of 28,800 bps is faster than a speed of 14,400 bps.

**byte** A measure of the amount of space that data takes up on a hard drive or a floppy disk. Consisting of eight bits, a byte can be thought of as a letter or a digit.

**CAR (computer-assisted reporting)** Reporting that uses software and hardware for a story.

**cartridge** In computers, the small tape cartridge that is rapidly replacing nine-track tapes.

**CD-ROM (compact disk, read-only memory)** A disk that contains up to 600 megabytes (600 million bytes) of information and looks just like a musical compact disk.

**cell** In a spreadsheet, a box containing information.

**codebook** A document translating codes used in a database. For example, the numeral 3 = black.

**database** A file or collection of related files.

**database manager** A software program that organizes information in columns and rows and makes it easy to search quickly, to total numbers by categories, and to link one file to another.

**disk** A floppy disk that is inserted into a computer. Used interchangeably with "diskette."

**DOS (disk operating system)** A system for operating an IBM personal computer.

**download** To transfer files to your own computer from a computer you have contacted over phone lines or through a network.

**EBCDIC (extended binary coded decimal interchange code)** Pronounced EB-SEE-DIC. The way IBM mainframes arrange the 0s and 1s that make up bytes. To use a file coded in EBCDIC on a personal computer, you need to translate it to ASCII with a software program.

**email (electronic mail)** A message sent electronically across networks and phone lines.

**field** A part of a record in an electronic database manager. Used synonymously with "column" or "cell" or "variable."

**FTP (file transfer protocol)** A program language that permits a user to transfer a file from one computer to another over the Internet.

**gopher** A language that allows a user to look at menus (organized lists) of files on other computers on the Internet.

**hard disk** Used interchangeably with "hard drive," the hard disk is the disk inside a computer on which files are stored.

**homepages** Screens of information on the World Wide Web that are linked by keywords to other screens.

**hypertext** Text files that have highlighted words. When a user places the cursor on the highlighted text (the "link") and clicks, he or she is automatically transferred to a file that contains additional information.

**Internet** A vast, worldwide, loosely arranged network of computers.

**listserv** A discussion group on the Internet on a particular subject. All messages sent to the listserv end up in the electronic mailboxes of those who have joined the listserv.

**log off** To tell a computer that you have finished using it.

**log on** To identify yourself as a user to a computer, telling it you want to use it.

**mainframe** A large, powerful computer usually kept in an isolated, air-conditioned room.

**mapping software** Software that provides maps, ranging from street addresses to countries. Other databases can be matched to those maps and the results visually represented by dots or shading.

**megabyte** A standard unit of measurement of computer files, representing approximately one million bytes. A 3.5-inch high-density disk contains approximately 1.4 megabytes.

**memory** The storage space on a computer. Generally refers to temporary space where programs run. Known as random access memory (RAM).

**modem (*modulator/de*modulator)** Equipment that allows a computer to use phone lines or other data transmission lines to contact other computers and the Internet.

**newsgroup** A group (reached through the Internet) that is formed to discuss a particular subject or interest.

**nine-track tapes** Large reels of magnetic tape, an outdated but common device used to store electronic information.

**observation** A record in statistical software, called a *row* in a spreadsheet.

**outliers** A record in a database that is either extremely small or large in relation to other records.

**PC (personal computer)** A computer that sits on a desktop; a smaller laptop computer. Also, usually refers to an IBM or an IBM-compatible desktop computer.

**RAM (random access memory)** The place on a computer where programs and files are temporarily stored. Most personal computers and Macintosh computers require 8 megabytes of RAM to run.

**record** A row of related information. Each distinct item of information appears in a separate column in that row.

**search tool** A program on the Internet that searches for information on the Web based on a word or phrase.

**spreadsheet** A software program used for calculations, budgets, and other number-related tasks.

**table** In a database manager, a table is a file in which information is stored in columns and rows.

**telnet** A program that allows you to connect to another computer and to use that computer's information or other resources.

**upload** To transfer files from your own computer to a computer you have contacted over phone lines or through a network.

**URL (uniform resource locator)** The address of a Web site. For example, the URL for the Census Bureau site is <http://www.census.gov>.

**variable** In statistical software, a category of information that is called a *column* in a spreadsheet and a *field* in a database manager.

**WAIS (wide area information server)** Pronounced WAYS. A program that allows a user to search the text of files on the Internet.

**Web browser** A program that allows you to view graphics and text on the World Wide Web.

**Windows** A widely used Microsoft operating system for the personal computer.

**World Wide Web** A service on the Internet that allows a user to use text, sound, and graphics files. The Web also lets you use hypertext on one computer to refer to a file on another computer.

**zip** To compress a file so that more information can fit on a disk or can be transmitted over a network or phone line.

## Acknowledgments

AltaVista screen shots. AltaVista and the AltaVista logo are trademarks or service marks of Compaq Computer Corporation. Reproduced with the permission of Compaq Computer Corporation.

The American Red Cross Web site <www.redcross.org>. © 1997 The American Red Cross. All rights reserved. Used with permission.

America Online screen shots. "America Online," "AOL" and the Logo design are all Registered Trademarks of America Online, Inc. Used with permission.

Deja News Quick Search screen shot. Used with permission.

Missouri Department of Natural Resources screen shots. Used with permission.

Netscape Netcenter Browser Frame. Copyright © 1998 Netscape Communications Corp. Used with permission. All Rights Reserved. This electronic file or page may not be reprinted or copied without the express written permission of Netscape. Netscape Communications Corporation has not authorized, sponsored, or endorsed, or approved this publication and is not responsible for its content. Netscape and the Netscape Communications Corporate Logos, are trademarks and trade names of Netscape Communications Corporation. All other product names and/or logos are trademarks of their respective owners.

ProfNet home page and Search query Web site. © ProfNet 1998. Used with permission.

WebCrawler and the WebCrawler Logo are trademarks of Excite, Inc. and may be registered in various jurisdictions. Excite screen display copyright © 1995–1998 Excite, Inc.

WinZip screen shots. Printed with permission of Nico Mak Computing, Inc.

Yahoo! screen shots. Text and artwork copyright © 1998 by Yahoo! Inc. All rights reserved. Yahoo! and the Yahoo! logo are trademarks of Yahoo! Inc.

# INDEX